cl⊙se
-ups

Close-Ups is a series of pocket guides to the world of film from *Little White Lies* and William Collins. In the title you are holding, our hope is that you find a fresh, personal exploration of a particular director, actor, movement or genre. We hope that you will join our authors in their efforts to look at movies through a new lens.

David Jenkins
Editor
Little White Lies Magazine

close-ups

VAMPIRE MOVIES

CHARLES BRAMESCO

WILLIAM
COLLINS

For Bram Stoker,
who gave us the night,
and Bram Norton,
who gave me the gene.

CONTENTS

INTRODUCTION

What sets the vampire apart from the werewolf, the zombie, the mummy and the rest of the frightful coterie that's paraded through horror cinema over the past century and change? The simple answer — and it's because the answer is not simple that the book now in your hands exists at all—is charisma. A vampire's got personality. The vampire has thoughts that go beyond "eat" or "kill" or "braaaaains". It's capable of surprising an audience, of having internal complexity that no walking killing machine can. Poke around in the strange psychological brew of sex and death from which the vampire emerged, and the figure might even start to look a little tragic.

But only sometimes. The vampire genus collects a wider variety of species than any other monster, appearing in all manner of shapes and sizes, with wildly inconsistent physical traits and abilities. Even a seven-foot rat-faced aberration like *Nosferatu*'s Count Orlok shares at least a few strands of DNA with the mute enchantress that Grace Jones portrays in *Vamp*. Set aside the creature in question, and little binds one vampire film to another; they've assumed all genres, all tones and covered every corner of the planet. This book attempts to survey the many subspecies of silver-screen vampire for a cinematic field guide, organizing the vast canon through criteria of style and content rather than a historical timeline. Use it as a practical resource on your own travels through cinema, directing you to a new path or illuminating the one you're already on.

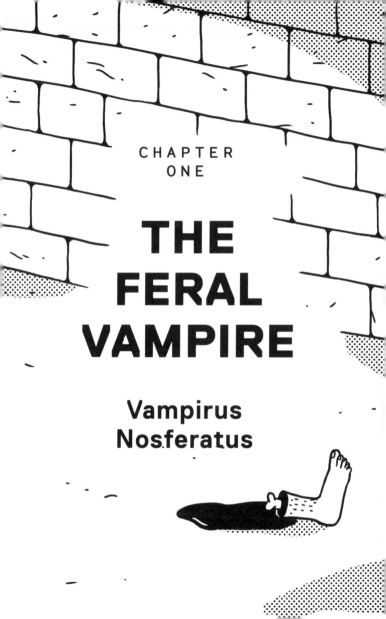

CHAPTER
ONE

THE
FERAL
VAMPIRE

Vampirus Nosferatus

Once upon a time in Weimar Germany, fledgling movie studio Prana Film needed a hit. Founder Albin Grau wanted to mount a project based on an idea a Serbian farmer had given him during his tenure in military service, about a man rising from the dead to walk the Earth and spread terror. Like most of Europe, he had read Bram Stoker's 1897 novel *Dracula* and figured that it would be as good a place as any to start. Grau and Prana cofounder Enrico Dieckmann soon contacted screenwriter Henrik Galeen with an unusual, specific assignment. There was no way that the still-green Prana would shell out to actually purchase the rights to adapt Stoker's book, so it fell to Galeen to alter the source material just enough to protect them from litigation, but not so much that the story and its crowd-pleasing villain would be rendered unrecognizable. The *Transformers* have no-budget imitator *Transmorphers*, and *Dracula* had *Nosferatu*; Galeen retained the particulars of Stoker's plot and the core elements of his title character, leaving no room for those familiar with the novel to mistake the fiend. But in order to legally cover both his and his employer's hindquarters, Galeen swapped out a couple of key names. He re-christened the villain Count Orlok, and bestowed upon the film a new title, taken from the script's hushed word alluding to "the bird of death": *Nosferatu.*

Cinema's first vampire was a rip-off.

(It bears mentioning that this did not work; representatives from Bram Stoker's estate sued the bejesus out of Prana and won in short order. A judge agreed that Galeen had jacked enough of Stoker's work to constitute copyright infringement, and ordered that all extant copies of the film be destroyed in addition to awarding a large monetary settlement. Prana went bankrupt immediately, unaware that a few unlicensed prints of their lone release had survived, getting preserved and re-duplicated by the cult fanbase that had sprung up around this singular picture. Having granted their medium one of its formative texts, the Prana founders retired as failures—that's showbiz.)

The V-word had been uttered as early into the film medium's infancy as the nineteen-teens, but always with obscure or archaic definitions. The "vamp," an old-fashioned term for a woman of loose morals and looser-fitting nightgowns, cropped up in

a handful of early reels under the label of vampire, most notable among them Robert Vignola's 1913 short *The Vampire*. Just as misleadingly titled was Louis Feuillade's French crime serial *Les Vampires*, which revolved around the illicit exploits of a fully human biker gang dubbed "the Vampires." Though it had a vague presence in the developing film form, the vampire didn't assume the shape we currently recognize it by until 1922, when, in an odd wrinkle of fate, the first true masterpiece of the bloodsucker-cinema canon was forged from the crucible of creative licensing complications.

Though he was nicknamed after a bird and shares a bit of DNA with the blood-feasting bat, Orlok's closest animal relative would still have to be the rat. From underneath the pancake make-up that gave him a sickly pallor all too fitting for the ghastly German Expressionist style, Schreck evinced a twitchy sense of unease reminiscent of vermin. Orlok's a freak and he knows it, leagues removed from the hypnotic smooth operator Dracula. Schreck's outward appearance splits the difference between man and beast: his bushy eyebrows, jam-packed mouthful of fangs, and majestically oversized honker coexist awkwardly, and Schreck's performance reflects that. He moves through each scene with a nervous tension, visibly fighting the urge to cut the foreplay and affix his mouth to his guest's jugular vein. Schreck's default pose involves folding his spindly fingers over his chest with a barely-suppressed anticipation—Murnau first introduces us to the character as he emerges from a shadowy half-tunnel, clutching his hands like a rodent. It's difficult not to imagine Germans at the *kino* a century ago, watching foolish solicitor Thomas Hutter approach Orlok's castle and bellowing that time-honored yet tragically futile warning, "Don't go in there!" (Or, rather, "*Geh doch nicht dahin!*")

Hard as he is to look at, Orlok still exudes a weird magnetism almost erotic in its intensity. Sex, curious parties will find, has always been mixed up in the foundational composition of the vampire, and Orlok drew a deeper connection to instinctual, biological drives than most. Long before he was transmogrified into a hirsute hunk with the chiselled jaw of Hugh Jackman for a 2004 solo film, Dr. Van Helsing was a typically bookish professor who educated the townspeople down the mountain from Orlok's castle. In *Nosferatu*, Professor Bulwer, Van Helsing's first iteration, shows his students an aggressive polyp and a venus flytrap ensnaring an unsuspecting fly. This tableau illustrates the natural principles of predator and prey, and, moreover, it frames up a clear pair of symbols for Orlok's consumptive need to feed. He regards blood with a reverence bordering on fetishistic, instantly rushing to suck on that poor bastard Hutter's hand when he inadvertently slices it at dinner. "Blood! Your precious blood!" Orlok cries, in one of his few lines of title-card dialogue. Orlok's figure casts him as an Other, and a repulsive one at that. But perversely, he taps into a part of the id liable to make the audience a little uncomfortable with its familiarity. The key to Orlok's disturbing sway over his audience lies in how he physically manifests his foreign bloodlust like a recognizable hunger, the point at which human self-awareness intersects with the bestial self-preservation drive.

Orlok is a primitive presence in his handsomely appointed home, sometimes incongruously so. He possesses enough mental

facility to formulate a plot to trap Hutter, and yet he's too closely linked with the coarser nature of the organism to fully qualify as anything close to human. This fundamental inhumanity makes Orlok fearsome, but it also makes him simple. As a narrative component, this abomination was potent, but not without his limits.

Count Orlok could only have been a product of the silent film era. Everything about the medium, its constraints in particular, suited this strain of vampire: he made sense as a largely silent character, allowed the occasional line of dialogue on interstitial title cards but mostly communicating via looming and staring. Leaving Orlok largely mute enhanced his mystique and reinforced his aura of unknowability, further estranging him from any remaining semblance of humanity. Monochrome photography also played to his strengths, emphasizing the harsh contrast between light and shadow, and lending him an even more gaunt look. The grotesquerie of Schreck's performance made perfect sense in the predominant mode of silent film acting, reliant on exaggerated expression to communicate what dialogue couldn't. But as indelible an impression that Orlok left, the cinematic vampire tradition would have to leave him behind to move forward.

As the film form evolved, the vampire mold would have to expand to allow for wider utility. Orlok cuts an imposing silhouette, and yet the primitive qualities that define the character couldn't allow for a complete range of feeling. Though Schreck stole the show, Orlok's really a minor character in his own story. Murnau was well aware that the character would be most effective when used sparingly, his absence and the sense of anticipation that it created proving more useful than overexposure would have been. Some of the most well-known icons of horror cinema spend most of their films lurking around the fringes; Pinhead barely appears in a few of the films branded under the *Hellraiser* franchise. But the vampire—and one Transylvanian dandy in particular—proved too charismatic a type to remain sidelined.

Future vampires would radiate charisma in a way that shuffling, uncomfortable-in-his-own-decomposing-skin Orlok never could. As a result, his quiet intensity sticks out like a long-nailed sore thumb in an era of color and sound. That's not conjecture, either; audiences witnessed the proof firsthand in 1979, when filmmaker/sage/madman/prophet of doom Werner Herzog unveiled his great tribute to Murnau's triumph, *Nosferatu the Vampyre.* The film doubled as an update to—and slavishly loyal remake of—Murnau's original, somehow bringing the material into the present while preserving it with absolute fidelity, as if within a museum exhibit.

Herzog kept his diversions from Murnau's method to a minimum, modernizing only where new advances could be applied naturally and

unobtrusively. For one, with legal squabbles far behind the property, Herzog could reinstate the official title of Dracula to Orlok. He reinvigorated the spartan Weimar-era designs with rich, earthy color, enlisted avant-electronica outfit Popol Vuh for a duly eerie score, and fed his ghoul grandiose soliloquies of pessimism typical of the famously grim director. "Time is an abyss profound as a thousand nights. Centuries come and go. To be unable to grow old is terrible, death is not the worst. Can you imagine enduring centuries, experiencing each day the same futilities?" would have been a lot to squeeze onto one title card. Even so, that's a pretty solid approximation of what Schreck's Orlok would have said, if he had had the space to do so.

But if Orlok is the soul of *Nosferatu*, then Herzog kept it fully intact by finding the second coming of Max Schreck in his longtime leading man Klaus Kinski, a performer with an unparalleled talent for alienation. With his pronounced lips, deep-set eyes, and overall cretinous energy, Kinski was perfect for the job of resurrecting the moldering corpse of the original vampire. He plays Orlok with the same quavering timidity that abruptly gives way to single-minded hunger, adding a slight edge of vulnerability by tucking his hair under a bulbous bald cap. This Orlok looks a bit more fleshy, a bit more frail, but he's the genuine article.

Herzog's faithful adaptation is an accomplished, splendorous film in its own right. Still, it can't help but illustrate how the dominant tastes of cinema had left behind Murnau's vision for his monster. To the modern-day viewer, *Nosferatu* is like Shakespeare: rich with intellectual merit, hugely formative to its canon, a formal wonder, but inextricable from its place in the past. And like many of Shakespeare's works, *Nosferatu* was born as an offering to the commoners, a crowd-pleasing work that could play to the basest tastes. At the time of its release, Herzog's lofty conflation of the sacred with a feral profane played more like a well-conceived art project than the scare-a-palooza that the Prana Film heads demanded of Murnau. That Orlok and Nosferatu's current stomping grounds encompass exhibitions and classrooms rather than grindhouses or B-movie archives speaks to Murnau's sheer mastery of his medium, but moreover, to how harshly its take on the vampire clashes with those that would follow. Measured against the conflicted, magnetic bloodsuckers who'd succeed him, the feral vampire feels more like a force than a proper character, generating a cool ambience over instantly gratifying scares.

By the turn of the millennium, Orlok and the feral-vampire archetype had been so thoroughly divorced from the mainstream that macabre-friendly filmmaker E. Elias Merhige could fully re-process Murnau's film as accented legend. Merhige's feature *Shadow of the Vampire* imagined the goings-on behind the scenes of *Nosferatu*, with an affected John Malkovich portraying F.W. Murnau as a tormented artist, opium addiction and all. But as ever, the film belongs to its villain: Schreck was reincarnated once more, this time in the hissing, beady-eyed form of esteemed creepazoid Willem Dafoe. And though Dafoe gave an earnestly committed performance as Schreck, Merhige guided it towards parody.

The film imagines that Schreck hid a bona fide case of vampirism beneath a guise of absolute Method acting, and that the cast and crew were unwittingly living a horror film even as they were helping to create the genre. As fun as Dafoe's sneering central turn is, it comes perilously close to

cartoon territory. "This is hardly your picture any longer," Schreck growls to a fuming Murnau, playing this vampire a little vampier than Murnau would have ever allowed. More in step with *The Addams Family* than Murnau's minimal interpretation, Merhige's affectionate mockery confirms that the feral vampire had been edged out of the realm of plausibility, useful to modern tastes primarily as a portal to the past.

Orlok's fate stuck him closer to obsolescence than extinction. While audiences have remained attached to the monstrous look of the vampire—the vampires slain by Buffy always assumed a facial mutation when preparing to feed—this specific type's reserved, even awkward gait has fallen out of fashion and prevented it from assuming a leading role. The feral vampire, a crude and impactful model, belongs to the past. But without it, the vast future that awaited Orlok's undead spawn would have been impossible.

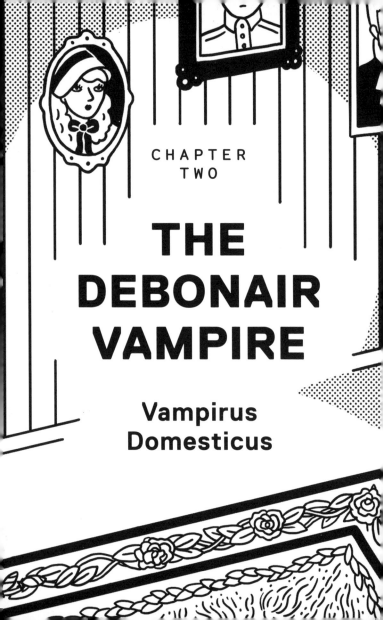

CHAPTER
TWO

THE DEBONAIR VAMPIRE

Vampirus Domesticus

Not once does Dracula speak the phrase "I want to suck your blood." It's his de facto catchphrase, the default sample text for the hammy impression that everyone seems to have. Even its enunciation and cadence have assumed icon status: the *w* curled into an Eastern European *v*, the double-*o* opening up to an overstated *ah*, the three bouncing emphases that fade out in the final syllable. And yet it's nowhere to be found in the 85 minutes of Tod Browning's 1931 film *Dracula*, only heard onscreen years later as parody of something that never really existed. Unlike the slightly-off nuisance of "Luke, I am your father," the bit is not a misquote or conflation of two lines, but a wholly invented figment.

It's a testament to the totality with which Bela Lugosi's debonair devil has permeated pop culture that the viewing public came up with an immortal soundbite for him. He captured the collective imagination and set off Hollywood's great love affair with franchising by merit of sheer popularity. Whether through the innumerable vampires that aped Browning and Lugosi's buttoned-up take or those that responded by challenging or otherwise subverting that same mythos, his influence cannot be overstated. He's life and death made one, classic and eternally current, so central to this course of lore that he's become a brand-name metonymy—the Band-Aid of vampires. He wants to suck our blood. His reputation precedes him.

The first Bram Stoker-sanctioned adaptation would arrive nine years after *Nosferatu*, flying proud and fully-licensed under the Dracula banner. To get technical about it, the very earliest film to dare invoke his name was 1921's *Drakula's Death*, a now-lost Hungarian silent whose insane asylum setting was but one of many divergences from Stoker's plot. There are murmurs among researchers of an even earlier project out of Russia, but a complete absence of filmstrips, records, or any other trace of existence suggests it may be apocryphal. Browning's feature represents the birth of the one true Dracula, the codification of the persona and style that would dictate the next century's perception of the vampire.

What's astonishing about Lugosi's performance is that he acts as if he already knows this. He steps in the room with the absolute self-assurance of someone aware that the audience loves them, as if he's waiting for the swell of studio audience applause that would break out whenever Kramer popped his head through Jerry Seinfeld's door.

Lugosi's Dracula lives theatrically, his every word, gesture, even step accentuated with an actorly panache. When Dracula lures the Thomas Hutter stand-in Renfield to dinner, he suggestively purrs "I never drink ... wine" for maximum effect. Like Dracula draining a helpless maiden's carotid artery, Lugosi milks every bit of business for all it's worth, theatrically recoiling from Renfield's mini-crucifix when the man slices his thumb with a steak knife. He basks in the adoration of a crowd that isn't there, drawing on the tradition of over-the-top facial

and in one of the stranger flourishes of set-dressing, stray armadillos scurry around Dracula's dining chamber, but the handsome Gothic architecture still clearly conveys wealth and class.

Allure is the animating force of Lugosi's Dracula, and that debonair vibe is absolutely essential to his dark work. Though contemporary standards of decency prohibited the display of anything explicit, Dracula's erotic pull is the lynchpin of his ability to mesmerize. Though his exploits would grow franker as the moviegoing public aged out of that prudishness, Lugosi still gives off a strong aura of sexuality. He shares Orlok's immediate arousal at the sight of blood, and yet Dracula can employ a lighter touch in his interactions with the fairer sex.

Part snake charmer and part pick-up artist, Dracula can claim ownership of a woman's heart (and nether regions) with a single glance. It's worth noting that his attacks posit a form of penetration, the fangs breaking the skin not radically dissimilar from the various insertions of sexual congress; vampirism is, by its very nature, sexualized. In contrast with later iterations of the vampire, however, Dracula's sexual expressions are restrained to the nebulous or connotative. We see him beckon to a trio of dolled-up women in

flowing nightgowns that the credits and Stoker's novel identify as Dracula's "brides," though their presence is fleeting and their interactions with Dracula practically nonexistent. Lugosi's Dracula is in full form when descending on the virginal Mina as she slumbers in a plush bed. After she tacitly offers herself to him over dinner, he claims his prize with the same unsettling combination of apprehension and anticipation as Humbert Humbert preparing to molest Lolita. Along with Dracula disintegrating in the morning light, the shot of Lugosi looming over his picture-perfect co-star Helen Chandler ranks as the most widely reproduced and imitated in the film. The image captures Dracula incarnate — high on bloodlust and regular lust, and even in the throes of a feeding frenzy, the very picture of composure.

The urbanity, internal contradiction, and human element of Lugosi's famed vampire all shone through when Dracula got its own *Shadow of the Vampire* with the Tim Burton-directed biopic *Ed Wood*. Just as Merhige's film did with Max Schreck, Ed Wood imagines the story behind the fiend with Martin Landau portraying an aged, washed-up, heroin-addicted Lugosi. The contrast between the two portrayals couldn't be tidier: where Dafoe literalized Schreck as a freak beyond the boundaries of human biology, Landau located and exposed the most vulnerable, humbling dimensions of Lugosi's personality. He plays the out-of-work actor as a hardened lump of self-pity. He resents the movie biz that left him behind, but allows the viewer a glimpse at hope and redemption when schlock-auteur Ed Wood's guileless enthusiasm reminds Lugosi of the magic of the pictures.

A smash hit from the outset, Lugosi's *Dracula* spawned a long string of sequels for Universal, some of them more tangential than others. Though Lugosi's name would remain synonymous with the Dracula character, he wouldn't reprise the role until 1948's *Abbott and Costello Meet Frankenstein*. Four films filled the 17 intervening years. *Dracula's Daughter* didn't even show the Count himself, instead casting Gloria Holden as a fetching descendant. Lon Chaney stepped in for *Son of Dracula*, John Carradine took over for *House of Frankenstein* and its companion piece *House of Dracula*, and way down the line in 1979, Universal gave Dracula another shot with a dead-on-arrival revival featuring Frank Langella. But the next major reincarnation of Dracula finally came in 1958, and when it did, Christopher Lee was out for blood.

After scoring a lucrative payday with a big-screen treatment of Mary Shelley's *Frankenstein*, British production outfit Hammer Films was eager to get another yank of the monster-movie cash-teat. Executives remembered Universal making a mint out of the Dracula property, and greenlit a new, slightly more outré take on the material. The negotiations with Universal for the rights to the character were long and complicated, to the point that production on Hammer's film began and reached completion before ink had dried on the 80-page contract. Christopher Lee's Dracula wasn't just faster, hungrier, and gorier; for a while, he was technically illegal.

Luckily—for Lee, Hammer, and us—the studios reached an agreement. and a little over a month later, the world bore witness to a lush, ferocious new vision for Transylvania's most famous resident. Director Terence Fisher brought an unprecedented new height of artistry to the property, enlivening 1958's *Dracula* as well as the sequels *The Brides of Dracula* (in which Lee did not appear, replaced by the same trio of groupies that cameoed in Lugosi's movie) and *Dracula: Prince of Darkness* with lurid color, gruesome practical effects, and opulent sets. Lee stuck around past Fisher's tenure, terrorizing regular foe Abraham Van Helsing through five more films, including the then-present-day-set *Dracula A.D. 1972*. Beyond the auspices of Hammer, Lee would star as Dracula once more, in Spanish filmmaker Jesus Franco's 1970 film *Count Dracula*. In Franco's film, Lee's Dracula actually ages backward, beginning as a gaunt husk of himself and regressing into his prime. It's an uncanny, ironic path for the final chapter of a role that saw Lee visibly aging as he played a character who was not supposed to.

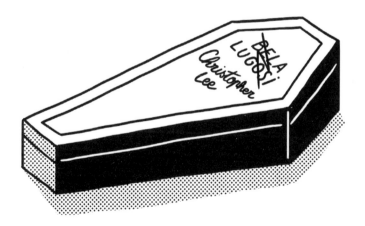

The Hammer films worked under the guiding aesthetic principle of "Dracula, but more," amplifying Universal's Gothic atmosphere with even more grandiose production design, then gussying it up with as much violence as the mid-century audience could stomach. The opening title card sees blood thinly spatter on a headstone marked Dracula, like a stream of red Day-Glo urine. It's an auspicious opening, and a warning to audiences with recollections of Lugosi that this would not be their father's Dracula.

Lee underscored the duality of the Dracula character in his performance. His Dracula plays up the mannered air of propriety bordering on pomp, and then contrasts it with a jagged, modern ferocity when possessed by hunger for a hemoglobin. This Dracula is a man of few words, but when he deigns to address his guests/victims, he speaks politely and articulately. He scans as a bit more rakish that Lugosi's ghoul; he takes a clear satisfaction in laying claim to vampire hunter Jonathan Harker's fiancée Lucy, implicitly cuckolding Harker by converting her to a vampire. (This film marks the first instance of Dracula possessing the ability to create new vampires, instead of merely psychically enslaving humans.) He's got the same flair for the dramatic, presenting himself to his guests at the top of a tall staircase, enshrouded in shadow with the requisite orchestral minor chord. He's the focal point of the shot that introduces him; he devours the frame.

And yet this Dracula was never able to evade an intrinsic coarseness of character. While later films pushed the envelope past the point of tearing, Fisher was regarded as a daring provocateur for depicting the character with fangs bared, blood staining his mouth like a child on a fruit punch bender. During his hunger-fuelled berserker state, Dracula's pupils dilate and his eyes take on a manic red glow. He's not so estranged from his humanity to verge on the Orlockian, but he's clearly subject to spells of possession typified by a subhuman thirst for carnage. Like the film in which he appears, he synthesizes the perfect fusion of high culture and low, of dignified Gothic literature and the scuzzy heritage of splatter cinema that would go on to cannibalize it.

Vampire cinema scholars (there are dozens of us!) tend to vaunt Fisher's Dracula pictures as the ideal midpoint between the accomplished-if-a-bit-sedate early films and the exploitation deluge of the '70s. This decade tested the full pliability of the Dracula figure, tweaking the character by

factor but with an undercurrent of admiration rather than mockery. (The film begins with a headstone projectile-vomiting black blood. Like Oldman's turn as Dracula, it starts out ridiculous and remains committed to its own schtick until it becomes somewhat disturbing.) Oldman's sumptuous performance functioned as commentary on Dracula as much as a manifestation of Dracula himself, reflecting the character's evolution into an idea or set of characteristics to be engaged with, rather than a type to be played straight. Even the failed films recognized the necessity of reconfiguring Dracula in some way; Gary Shore's 2014 would-be franchise-starter *Dracula Untold* limply imagined the vampire as a gritty, tormented antihero, complete with bat-themed superpowers for an age dominated by spandex-clad blockbusters.

It's nearly unwatchable, and the conclusive proof that the Dracula fields had been plowed to aridity. Dracula can't go home to Transylvania to frighten intrepid real estate contract agents any longer, he can only drift from interpretation to interpretation. Stoker's original text has grown as canonized as the Bible, a timeless slate onto which modern trends and ideas can be projected. Even those Draculas hewing on the side of tradition stick out for their devoutness, that adherence to classical form an interpretive choice nonetheless.

The years following Lee's Dracula stint would see this archetype splinter and mutate, spawning a whole teeming menagerie of vampire subspecies presenting responses, refutations, and remixes of the vampire narrative's Rosetta Stone. Dracula has remained, to an extent, an immutable quantity: we see his face, and no matter how many revisionist takes we've watched, we know instinctively that he wants to suck our blood. But as the creative floodgates began to swing open, the vampire organism was set on a track towards an explosion of biodiversity.

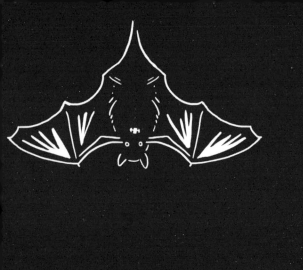

CHAPTER
THREE

THE CLOWN VAMPIRE

Vampirus Comidicus

Abbott and Costello Meet Frankenstein, ground zero for the unholy cinematic fusion of humour and horror, is that rarest and most gratifying of films: a good idea in spite of itself. On paper, everything about it reeks of tin-eared conglomerate brand synergy. Universal had widely beloved comedy duo Bud Abbott and Lou Costello on the payroll in 1948, and reasoned that the most cost-effective use of their talents would be to pair them with some of the old intellectual property they had lying around. In an elaborate display of franchise-jockeying, Universal revived the Wolfman, reanimated Frankenstein's monster, and even persuaded Bela Lugosi to take up Dracula's cape once again, all for a madcap mash-up of laughs and chills bound together by corporate parentage. Costello pegged the idea as hackish after reading a first draft, reportedly scoffing, "No way I'll do that crap. My little girl could write something better than this."

One pay bump later, he was on set and proving himself wrong. Casting Abbott and Costello as a pair of bumblers out of their genre's element would prove to be a stroke of genius, and the film made enough money to spawn a whole series in which they made the acquaintance of various ghouls. The peerless physical comedians treated the schematic of the creature feature as their personal playset, inserting themselves into a stock horror narrative (they portray a pair of foolhardy freighters who accidentally release a menagerie of monsters and take it upon themselves to get them back) and tearing a swath of havoc through every scene. Importing slapstick into the milieu of the macabre was a cinch for the leads, the expression of "abject terror" a natural fit for Costello's tittering neurotic style. But while the chemistry between Abbott and Costello made them superstars and essentially carried the whole of their encounter with Universal's stable of phantoms, they enjoyed no such rapport with Bela Lugosi's returning Dracula.

Abbott and Costello's act merely takes place within the location of a horror film, rather than integrating the trappings of the genre on a conceptual level. Their double-take sight gags, for instance, could be transplanted into another one of their many comedy vehicles with little difficulty. As the title suggests, it's Abbott and Costello as the audiences knew and loved them, plopped into a new set of circumstances. That meant, however, that Dracula was not permitted to get in on the fun. He's forced to play the straight man against Abbott and

to mold Dracula into a fresh shape. These films broke new ground in terms of the genre territory staked out, but it wasn't until the next decade that the new breed of vampire would surface in earnest.

The '70s saw the emergence of a vampire that could loosen up and live a little, a riff on known lore with an added dash of fun ranging in tinge from light whimsy to full-bore mania. Bram Stoker's original myth provided lots of comic cannon fodder for irreverent parody, as a spate of films seized on the naturally hilarious contrast between the stodgy centuries-old setting of Dracula and the baffling modernity in which it was forced to live on. A minority did so symbolically; rather than fully wresting Dracula from the context of his story, unofficial King of the Borscht Belt Mel Brooks imposed a modern comedic sensibility on him with 1995's uproarious farce *Dracula: Dead and Loving It.*

Brooks stuck to the same core beats of Stoker's novel, but crammed schticky gags into every spare beat available—he's essentially doodling mischievous cartoons in the margins of a leather-bound book like it was an issue of *MAD Magazine.* In one scene, snivelling servant Renfield's attempt to discreetly eat an insect turns into him scarfing a spider out of the air and slurping its web up like fettuccine. In another, Stoker creation Dr. Seward prescribes enemas as an absolute and unquestionable cure-all. In the most over-the-top bit of the film, Jonathan's reluctant staking of a vampire-converted Lucy generates enough geysers of blood that the overkill works as a joke in itself. But the main course is Leslie Nielsen as the man himself, offering a Dracula that's a study in contrasts. He wants to be the perfectly-pressed Count, irresistible to all living souls, but Nielsen's goofball routine proves irrepressible and undermines his aura of authority. His first introduction perfectly encapsulates the comic alchemy at work in Brooks' film: he appears in the darkness at the top of a staircase, assuming the same portentous position as Lugosi's original, a tableau worthy of that oft-abused descriptor "iconic," but Nielsen then spoils the moment by slipping on a pile of faeces and falling on his face down the rest of the stairs.

Nielsen's take on Dracula splits the difference between a Friars' Roastmaster and the pop-culture referents Brooks relies on the audience to recognize. In some instances, the humor goes more specifically allusive; the audience won't chuckle at the oddly-shaped hairpiece Nielsen plucks off his head unless they're familiar with Oldman's mighty coif from Bram Stoker's *Dracula*. (Though it's impossible not to at least crack a smile at his inversion of the essential line: "I never drink ... wine. Aw, what the hell, let me try it!") But in a more general sense, he puts corny slants on all of Dracula's most essential traits, creating a new and antithetical take on the vampire and what it represents.

If the vampire is made of sex and death, seducing the human (both its victim and the viewer) by assuaging our fear of decomposition with eternal virile life, Nielsen offers an alternative lacking only the glamor. He still possesses all the same powers of Dracula — the hypnotic suggestion, transmogrification into a bat, the ability to infect others with the vampiric germ—and yet they all seem to be on the fritz, subverting the vampire's crucial collected air. He can bend an unfortunate usher to his will, but the ambiguities of language render her an ineffective servant and leave Dracula dumbfounded at her incompetence, which is to say, his own incompetence. Nielsen allows Dracula no sense of restraint, no suggestive implication to his actions. Brooks recreates the scene wherein Renfield cuts his thumb, but instead of swooping to the open wound in the manner of Lugosi or Schreck, Nielsen smacks his lips like a cartoon dog eyeing a juicy ribeye. He's in possession of what a younger generation of reader would define as "no chill." And, somewhat improbably, having that very same chill is what makes the vampire an object of fearsome fascination.

Nielsen and Brooks' spin on the material makes the daring suggestion that the implausible aspect of Dracula is not his supernatural powers, but rather his imposing screen presence. Brooks converts a frightening quantity into a laughable one by exposing the specific quality of menace endemic to vampires as antiquated. Dracula's aristocratic air scans as ludicrous when contrasted with the coarseness and candour of modern speech and tastes.

This comic interplay between the past and present persisted in most of the comic vampire's onscreen occurrences, with the rift being torn open even wider once the Dracula of yore was dragged into modern times. Brooks struck gold by lending the character a 20th-century streak of irony, but during the '70s-era boom times, films on the fringes took the concept further and chrono-ported him to the date of release completely unchanged. When Abbott and Costello met him in their fish-out-of-water comedy, Dracula was the dry land onto which the fish had flopped; in such films as *Vampira* and *Love at First Bite*, he was the one in need of water. These satires plopped Dracula into the age of disco and updated his lecherous tendencies into a good-natured horniness befitting the era (in one film, he pursues a supermodel; in another, a Playboy bunny), but no film reckoned with the mythology and archetypes of vampire fiction with as much deconstructive brio as *What We Do in the Shadows*.

Taika Waititi—once an eccentric indie filmmaker busying himself with curious genre projects in his native New Zealand, now the Marvel Studios HR department's latest acquisition—sank his teeth into what had, by that point, become clichés of the vampire subgenre with his 2014 mockumentary. A camera crew chronicles the goings-on between four flatmates in a suburb of Wellington, and the assorted specimens of the comic vampire pay homage to well-known archetypes rooted in archaic myth. Eastern European lothario Vladislav corresponds most closely to Dracula, the 8,000-year-old Petyr doubles for Count Orlok, foppish dandy Viago is of a piece with Oscar Wilde's heyday, and self-fashioned "young rebel" Deacon never aged out of the 19th century, a spring chicken at 183 years old. Waititi sets the living relics on a collision course with the world of 2014, and gets his laughs from the resultant friction.

Waititi logically concludes that centuries of remaining indoors during daylight hours and only slinking out of the isolated mansion in the nighttime would have mostly—not entirely, crucially—kept the vampires frozen in time. They get enough snatches of the now to make their macabre living situation resemble something akin to Real World: Transylvania Goes New Zealand, but they're unable to fully acclimatize to the progress beyond their walls. Waititi's comic conceit is situated in the gap between their Grand Guignol antiquity and the nonchalant, banal modernity, pitting the vampires against a human culture that has enough familiarity with their kind to no longer find them especially horrifying.

The comic vampire is identified not by his own characteristics, but the reaction they draw from those characters around them. Deacon keeps a human servant named Jackie, and because his commands tend to involve picking up dry-cleaning or tidying the house rather than anything of Renfieldian morbidity, she regards him like an employee would a jerk boss. (In the single most succinct critical analysis of vampire fiction on record, she describes Deacon and his posse as "one big homoerotic dick-biting club.") Even less impressed by the vampires is Nick, a thickheaded doofus Jackie brings to their lair as a snack, only for him to join their ranks. Even when in mortal peril, he acts nonplussed, and mainly treats his own vampirism like a cool trick to be bragged about at bars. He's everything the main characters aren't, the casual counterpoint to their baroque lifestyle.

Petyr's pretty much set in his ways, but over the course of the film, the three others begin to embrace the technology and manners of their present. This offers Waititi ample opportunity for takeoffs of vampire pop-culture detritus; one line goes so far as to name-check *The Lost Boys*, and, in another, Vladislav hisses the classic line "leave me to my bidding!" in reference to a competitive eBay auction for a table. By imposing vampiric lore on a disillusioned age, Watiti drains all the hot air from the core trio to leave them as nothing more imposing than touchy, temperamental recluses. The film's funniest joke also serves as a microcosm of its satirical apparatus: Deacon confides that "I think we drink virgin blood because it sounds cool," and Vladislav helpfully elaborates, "I think of it like this: if you are going to eat a sandwich, you would just enjoy it more if you knew no one had fucked it."

When a film plays its vampires for laughs rather than the usual terror, the various characteristics giving the character an oxygen-draining screen presence turn into odd peccadillos. Waititi dares to acknowledge the senselessness of the vampire by stating its identity in plain and sober terms. And as one inspects this cadre of haughty fools more closely, the irony of their film's title comes into focus: the vampire can only thrive in shadow, where the immediate distraction of fright can obscure its more risible details, and Waititi's film floods their decrepit mansion with a documentary crew's floodlights to tease a certain childishness out of their habits. The fact of the matter is that most of what vampires do boils down to bonus points for the cool factor: how they dress, how they wear their hair, how they talk, they way they select and entrance victims. The debonair quality of Dracula is merely the old-fashioned forebear to our modern sense of coolness, and though Vladislav, Deacon, and Viago had trouble pulling it off—both because the Dracula 'look' has long since gone out of fashion in our present, and because they're just plain bad at it — a generation of younger, hungrier vampires was waiting to take their place. And they had the leather jackets to make the look work.

Living my BEST After-life.

CHAPTER
FOUR

THE
COOL
VAMPIRE

Vampirus
Nihilisticus

The vampire can be most commonly found stalking the annals of literature, horror cinema, and the occasional nightmare, but in the latter half of the 20th century, its dominion bled into the real world. In her revelatory 1999 book *Piercing the Darkness: Undercover with Vampires in America Today*, researcher Katherine Ramsland blew the lid off of an expansive and vibrant subculture flourishing in the major cities of the United States. Her exposé paints a shocking portrait of a hidden community where self-proclaimed vampires actually consume human blood in members-only clubs (the medical necessity of which remains a topic of hot debate), engage in what can be modestly described as 'exotic' sex acts oriented around feeding, and even keep slaves under the signature hypnotic spell. The dozens of smaller factions making up today's vampire underground differ on how they'd like to be regarded by mainstream society. Some make an effort to follow their unusual diet in the most peaceable way possible; more malevolent others are rumored to be responsible for the disappearance of Katherine Walsh, a journalist who was working on a scrapped precursor to Ramsland's book prior to her vanishing. But a few commonalities bind the groups together.

On a purely superficial level, modern vampiredom does the cultural work that *What We Do in the Shadows* comically avoids by updating its traditional aesthetics to the present day. The capes, pressed tuxedo shirts, and other formalwear are officially out, and a gloomy, grungy pastiche of Goth and punk styles is in. Rangy, asymmetrical hair has replaced the slicked-back Dapper Dan look, and dominant textiles include black leather, form-fitting synthetics, and flexible metal. Body modification isn't all that uncommon, with the more dedicated vampires donning colored contact lenses and ersatz fangs, and using makeup to give their skin that "just-been-slaughtered" non-glow.

The sartorial choices speak to a more purposeful ethos undergirding the vampire lifestyle as a whole. The BDSM-inflected outfits, the establishment of a specialized vernacular ("haemolacria," also known as the phenomenon of weeping blood, is a handy five-dollar word to bust out at cocktail parties) and the self-cordoning into insular chapters all signal a desire to break out of the restrictions of polite society. This distinct style works as a visual shorthand for individual rebellion—under the criteria of scholar Joel Dinerstein, author of *The Origins of Cool in Postwar America*, the key hallmarks of a bid at that slipperiest of social concepts. The modern punk vampire is, in essence, a flipped script: rather than travelling to a past wherein Dracula would be considered 'cool,' it retrofits the debonair vampire figure to an era so that his signifiers of cool make sense within a new context.

in the off-beat suburb of Santa Carla, where freak flags proudly fly ("people are strange when you're a stranger," teases the opening soundtrack cut, an Echo and the Bunnymen cover of The Doors), the local gang of devil-may-care ne'er-do-wells sets the standard for social capital. Feared and respected, they'd run the town even if they weren't draining it after sundown. They superimpose the magnetism of the vampire onto that of the classical bad-boy archetype; Michael is inexorably drawn to them even as their sharper edges frighten the fundamentally good kid.

The Lost Boys puts a savvy spin on the stock teen-fiction narrative of the upstanding protagonist who falls in with the wrong crowd, and in doing so, is himself changed. But the appeal of fitting in with the cool kids has a supernatural pull for Michael, and it falls to his younger brother Sam (Corey Haim) to save his soul—both literally and figuratively. Schumacher situates vampirism as the ultimate realization of the James Dean fantasy, enabling the affected to flout consequences for their actions and buck society's judgement more fully than anyone else. Michael's assimilation into the vampire clan is driven by a conscious desire to belong as much as it is by the invisible pull of hypnosis, or by Michael's crush on David's kept girl Star (Jami Gertz).

That erotic drive can't be without its corresponding death-drive, and Schumacher finds the vampiric embrace of death dovetails nicely with the teenage delusion of indestructibility. The film's defining scene places Michael and the vampires on a rickety railroad bridge, dangling from the tracks above a foggy gorge. As a train roars above them, the vampires drop one by one into the unknown below. David beckons to Michael to drop down, and the gesture is freighted with meaning. Between the two of them, it's a measure of faith and solidarity, a display of trust in David's leadership and a way to prove one's bona fides within the group. In a more symbolic sense, the flirtation with death hints at the group's nihilistic foundations. It's a flashier equivalent to smoking a cigarette. As succinctly stated in the tagline, these vampires have shrugged off any system of belief beyond the pursuit of hedonistic pleasure. And in that moment, Michael thumbs his nose at his own mortality and submits to his new entourage's live-fast die-never ethos. Shortly thereafter, he's baptized in blood when he drinks from a proffered bottle, and his transformation is set in motion.

The film's closing line—"One thing about living in Santa Carla I could never stomach: all the damn

vampires!" —is classic, but a slightly glib cop-out from the deeper implications of its plot. Michael's estimation of being a vampire only sours when he's called upon to go through the gory initiation of murder; he shies away before he gets the chance to fully grapple with the realities of life beyond death. *The Lost Boys* epitomized a romantic view of the punk vampire as a rebel free to live outside of ethics. It's not for nothing that the film joins David and his cronies as they're still teenagers, however, basically in the nascency of their vampire lifespan. After the millennium, a film offering an added dose of perspective would thoroughly gut this myth of vampire cool—while re-proving it beyond a shadow of a doubt.

Jim Jarmusch's 2014 film *Only Lovers Left Alive* begins trapped in a spiral. His camera whirls around and around, first melting the star-dotted cosmos into flecks of dust revolving on a vinyl record. From there, the frame continues to spin as it fades to reveal twinned vampires in a state of exhaustion and stasis, lovers continents apart but bonded by a quantum-physical connection. A woman, Eve (Tilda Swinton), splayed atop a makeshift throne of books in Tangier; a man, Adam (Tom Hiddleston), draped across a plush couch in Detroit with a wooden lute laying in his lap. The whole world's moving in circles, going nowhere, repeating itself.

It's a canny visual metaphor for the worldview of Adam, who's grown jaded and depressed from centuries of watching humanity trudge through the same cycles of self-sabotage. From his bird's-eye view of the ages, humanity is intent on destroying itself, having persecuted and executed history's greatest thinkers while hurtling towards a manmade environmental apocalypse. Adam sneeringly refers to humans as "zombies," and their gross perversions of art and science disgust him. He's obsessed with analogue technology, proudly showing off the DIY motor he cobbled together from found parts and cluttering his home with transistors and cathode ray tubes. He nearly dry-heaves at the prospect of

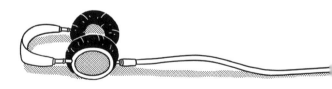

reducing something as intimate and personal as a music recording to a digitized download.

His residence in Detroit is all too apropos, too, as Jarmusch's lovingly shot decay of the once-bustling urban center acts as a towering symbol of failure and squandered potential. Adam remembers the city as a thriving hub of the auto industry and the cradle of blues, rock, and Motown. The only time he ventures out from his self-imposed seclusion in a Victorian-era house packed to bursting with bric-a-brac is for silent nighttime constitutionals around the city streets to gaze in resignation at the derelict buildings and think back on what was once there. Adam's not hermetically sealed from the onward march of time to *What We Do In The Shadows*'s extent—he's aware of the outside world, but rejects

it. He sees kinship with White Stripes frontman Jack White, another old soul out of joint with a hectic, crass present.

The film joins him as his despair reaches suicidal levels and he sends his Renfield-esque flunky portrayed by the late Anton Yelchin out in search of a wooden bullet. (Yelchin's character, by the way, is one of a handful of well-placed nods to past vampire classics from pop-culture packrat Jarmusch; on a plane, Eve does her own rendition of the "cut finger at the dinner table" scene from *Nosferatu*.) At the end of his rope, he feels he's seen enough to know that there's nothing worth living for. The essence of Adam's character is tied up in a pair of bleak ironies; the first is that living forever would necessarily create the desire to die.

The second is that Adam only gets cooler the more aggressively he shrugs off the label. All this fixation on the rot of progress makes him sound like a fogeyish get-off-my-lawn type, and while he does literally scare some kids off his lawn in one scene, Adam is deliberately fashioned as an emblem of cool. Jarmusch attires him in the standard-issue punk uniform, a less flamboyant take on the *Lost Boys'* costuming closet, all distressed black threads and Ray-Ban sunglasses. Adam's used his centuries on Earth to build up an encyclopedic knowledge of music and then put it to work on haunting prog compositions that wouldn't be out of place in an episode of *Twin Peaks*. His hypnotic body of work, along with the atmosphere of mystery he's attained by penning himself up at home, has earned him reluctant underground fame among in-the-know rock kids. As his assistant astutely notes, his efforts to be left alone have only garnered more attention; existentially spent, he can only reply with the passively negative, "What a drag."

Jarmusch has made a career out of pinpointing the soul-sickness beneath paragons of postured style. With *Only Lovers Left Alive*, he applies the same deconstruction of cool to the vampire type that he previously brought to the jailbird in *Down By Law* and the ladykiller in *Broken Flowers*. The director's interpretation of the vampire organism's abilities and limits hints at his thematic underpinnings — his characters scoff at garlic allergies or supernatural force-fields preventing them from entering homes uninvited. They are able to move with unnatural speed, and yet Jarmusch paints vampirism as something closer to an illness than a superpower. Decorum forces Adam and Eve to score their blood from doctors loosening up on the Hippocratic Oath,

and Jarmusch reinforces the dealer-junkie dynamic by shooting a sip of blood like a heroin rush, the camera lurching onto the floor as the user feels the relief wash over them.

Jarmusch would never deny that it's cool to be a vampire, but he amends the idea with its corollary that pain is the cost of being cool. Adam gets a foil when Eve senses his despondence and travels to Detroit to talk him off the proverbial ledge, and the closest this plot-light movie gets to an antagonist is

Eve's rambunctious new-in-town sister Ava (Mia Wasikowska). The three of them form a superego-ego-id arrangement, with Adam mired in his own thoughts, Eve sharing his weariness but assuaging it with an appreciation of life's pleasures, and Ava in a state of hungriness and horniness throughout the entire film, all wanton consumption. Ava would fit right in with the *Lost Boys* crew, still jittery with the excitement of being a vampire, not yet aware of the toll that time will exact on her. Adam knows better.

But while Jarmusch is sympathetic to Adam's withdrawal in disgust, he doesn't fully subscribe to it. "How can you have lived for so long and still not get it?" Eve asks Adam. "This self-obsession is a waste of living. It could be spent on surviving things, appreciating nature, nurturing kindness and friendship, and dancing. You have been pretty lucky in love though, if I may say so." She sees the value in going on, even if dust is the final fate of all creation. Cloistering yourself in a fortress of esoterica may be good for indie-rock bona fides, but the detachment it creates will corrode the soul.

Jarmusch takes vampirism as seriously as the real-world vampires that mimic Adam's style and disaffected demeanor. The director views the vampire as a tragic figure rather than the funhouse spook featured in "Soul Dracula," a silly clip from '70s French television that Ava watches in one scene. His brand of cool vampire, a portrait of chilly stoicism and world-weary disillusionment, rebuts any romanticized perceptions by detailing the ugly morass of anxiety over impermanence. That unease over transience, whether of the self or of the world they're doomed to outlive, is what causes that same disaffection.

But there was one vampire cooler than them all, whose social context gave his existence a sense of purpose that would turn Adam and Eve's grey skin green with envy. He had greater cause than any to withdraw from the world in disgust, having acutely and intimately suffered the cruelties of man. And yet he visibly and publicly weaponized his coolness, positioning it against a society that hated and feared him for being more than a vampire. A hint: he was black, and his name rhymed with Dracula.

CHAPTER
FIVE

THE
BLACK
VAMPIRE

Vampirus
Africanus

The realms of sci-fi and horror have long served as ready vessels for subtextual social commentary too sensitive to be baldly stated in a straightforward dramatic setting. It's simple and potent enough for a director to pinpoint a shared cultural anxiety and project it onto something scary or unfamiliar to smuggle in a charged statement on a hot-button issue. Aliens, robots, monsters, and ghosts all beg for a nice, juicy metaphor, to the point that audiences have gotten underwhelmed with genre films that don't endeavor to say much more than what's on their surface. And the vampire, in particular, offers fertile seeding ground for symbolism and insinuation.

The '70s saw a boom in so-called "blaxploitation" pictures, funk-soundtracked films made by, for, and about the black community. The trend's tentacles reached the horror tradition in 1972 with William Crain's *Blacula*. While the title character is indeed a vampire, he's not just a clone of Bram Stoker's creation with a higher melanin count. Rather, he's an enemy: in the opening scene, Prince Mamuwalde of the proud Abani nation meets with Drac himself to discuss putting an end to the slave trade between Eastern Europe and Africa. Dracula's a real jerk about things, not only well. A white coroner makes an off-color remark to the black detective hot on Mamuwalde's trail, and then refers to him using a slur as soon as he's out of earshot; later on, a cop leaps to the assumption that the Black Panthers were responsible for an unsolved murder. Bigotry is all but in the air.

In a more general sense, the black vampire type speaks to white America's contradictory combination of fear and desire for black strength, skill and potency. Even in the most deep-seated white prejudices, there's a fetishistic envy for the black body and its capabilities; black excellence is vaunted in athletics and performance, and minimized in more cerebral pursuits such as the sciences or academia. Mamuwalde awes those around him through the vampire's classic hypnosis, and naturally, their rapture emerges through physical and sexual channels. The likes of *Shaft*'s John Shaft and *Superfly*'s Youngblood Priest locked up triflin' suckas by day and spent their nights making sweet love to a rotation of grateful be-Afroed ladies. Like fellow blaxploitation icons, Mamuwalde's libido is the key component in his overall life force — his mojo, as it were.

But as much as typifying the defiant, prideful, undeniable ideal of black manhood in the '70s

empowered Mamuwalde, it partially hamstrung him as well. Maybe it was the robust muttonchops connecting his mustache to his head-hair like a black Chester Alan Arthur, maybe it was how stupidly perfect the portmanteau of the film's title was, but something about Blacula made it into a caricature of itself over the following decade. The character began with noble intentions, as Marshall himself spoke to the producers about reshaping the part to keep it dignified and meaningful to black viewers, independently renaming "Arthur Brown" to Mamuwalde and adding his royal background. Though the character began as a villain that underserved audiences knew they could safely believe in, the sequel *Scream Blacula Scream* lost sight of the character's bigger picture when it arrived the next year. The film muddles Mamuwalde's magisterial appeal by burying it under a cavalcade of needless subplots and other diversions, wronging him mainly in leaving him less space to be himself. The real killer was the plague of films that similarly appended "black" onto horror franchises as hasty cash-ins. The likes of *Blackenstein* and *Dr. Black, Mr. Hyde* punch-line-ified the original and stagnated the advance of the black vampire film — though not completely.

Eight months after *Blacula* doubled its budget at the box office and brought low-rent studio AIP a sorely needed windfall, Bill Gunn's otherworldly, radical *Ganja and Hess* spent a week in a single New York theater before it was pulled due to disinterest. A grave injustice, yes, but it's not all that difficult to see where the moviegoers of 1973 were coming from. The film is willfully difficult to access, eschewing the typical structure of horror and frequently indulging in experimental interludes that were more at home at the Cannes Film Festival, where an early print won the Critics' Choice prize. Most critically, Gunn did not share his colleague Crain's mission to give the black cinema canon an antihero that could make danger an admirable quality. His intentions lay elsewhere, in more pointedly critical territory.

Gunn saw the vampire's outcast nature as a ready analogue for the struggles of the black population's assimilation in a country that repeatedly insisted it had no place for them. When we first meet Dr. Hess Green (Duane Jones), he's an upper-crust intellectual with the palatial manor to match. He's a picture of success on his own terms, cluttering his home with African artifacts that connect him to his roots and show he hasn't grown into a "house negro," a term left over from the era of

American slavery referring to a neutered black man who accepts affluence in exchange for subservience to white owners. (Hess has a butler of his own, who the film treats with a rather puzzling scorn.) He's carved out his own corner of the American dream, and jeopardizes it all when his assistant George (played by Gunn himself) bungles a murder-suicide with an accursed African knife and turns Hess into one of the undead.

CHAPTER FIVE   103

His spiral takes off from there, and along a trajectory all too common to inner-city narratives. The thirst for blood hits Hess like an addiction that threatens to undo his entire life, driving him to theft and violent crime unbecoming for a gentleman of his stature. But unlike Jarmusch in *Only Lovers Left Alive*, Gunn takes the comparison between the need for blood and chemical dependency as symptomatic of social causes, rather than existential ones. When George's unknowing widow Ganja arrives at Hess' digs in search of her missing husband, Hess claims her, first as a lover and then as his companion in vampirism. This sets off a complex sequence of code-switching, as the title couple carefully navigates their new lives of violence while continuing to cling to their bourgeois facade. They're torn between identities, fielding diametrically opposed pressures from their own visceral urges and the harsh strictures of public judgement.

The topic of negotiating fractured identity is also at the heart of the *Blade* films, which dressed up the black vampire in a cross between superhero spandex and bondage gear. Starting in 1998, Wesley Snipes portrayed "daywalker" Eric Brooks, a human-vampire hybrid acting as the conduit between a clan of hawkish pureblood vampires and the human mainstream. While both sides itch for war, the hunter known as Blade forcibly maintains a ceasefire by staking the more radical sects of vampires, which have branded him as a highly wanted traitor. The series plays up Blade's dichotomous nature with the constant visual motif of sharp contrasts between light and shadow, often cloaking Snipes in darkness to set the mood of a moment or even change the shape of his face. Across the trilogy, characters alternately respect and distrust Blade for being the only one able to walk in the day and the night.

The cultural crossfire in which Blade gets caught corresponds to the same plight previously broached in 1934's "message picture" *Imitation of Life*: that mixed-race persons may be denied a sense of belonging, left searching for full acceptance on either side of their lineage. Those with one black parent and one white stick out among Caucasian crowds, and run the risk of getting rejected as lesser-than by peers with two black parents. The persisting, deleterious dismissal of "too black to be white, not black enough to be black" syncs up snugly with Blade's split genetic makeup. Moreover, he prizes his multifaceted persona. Blade regularly takes a special serum to remain in touch with his

human side and forestall his transformation into a full vampire. Taking the dose visibly pains him; inhabiting the middle isn't easy.

Guillermo del Toro, a Mexican filmmaker who knew a thing or two about vampires from his debut film *Cronos* (see chapter 10), took the reins of the *Blade* franchise for its second installment. He guided the property to new highs of aestheticized action, and in terms of the film's racially coded content, del Toro diversified the black vampire one step further with the introduction of Reapers. Ubervampires who drink the blood of human and vampire alike, the violent Reapers see Blade as the ultimate delicacy. Those so inclined can take them as a stand-in for extremist groups reserving contempt for anyone that doesn't join their doctrine of total upheaval, whether they be black, white or mixed-race. Again, Blade must play both sides against the middle, a man without a place, be it racial or genetic. The films would be mournful, if they weren't so hopped-up on a cocktail of speed and spiked blood.

Somewhat less concerned with promoting a lucid, progressive treatise on the politics of race was *A Vampire in Brooklyn*, a 1995 horror film directed by Wes Craven but starring, co-written, up as a model of disruption and then failing at his own game. Among the more memorable sequences finds Maximillian morphing into a corpulent church leader (Murphy donned a fat suit for the role-within-a-role, in a sad portent of such failures to come as *The Nutty Professor* and *Norbit*) and swindling his congregation into believing the only good parts of life are "evil" and "ass." The moment brings more confusion than laughs, because it's hard to tell who's the butt of the joke. The vampire's power of suggestion makes it look like the churchgoers are mindless sheep swayed by a few heated words with a flashy delivery, but of course Maximillian's the villain. Whether Murphy is railing against charlatans in the church or calling out black populations as easily manipulated by the same is not clear. A scene following Maximillian as he dances for no reason through an alleyway to "No Woman, No Cry" offers a mite of clarity; Murphy's just having fun with it. He's not here to save the world, and he gladly leaves the job to someone who's interested.

Maybe that was for the best, too, considering how hazardously fraught future bids at an enlightened black vampire cinema would be. The question of intersectionality dealt the genre a hurdle it stumbled while clearing. 1986's *Vamp* and 2002's *Queen of the Damned* might as well be sister films, linked in their ambition to address not only black tribulation, but black female tribulation. Each film places an icon whose celebrity stretched far beyond the confines of the silver screen onto a pedestal of worship. *Vamp* and *Queen of the Damned* exalt fashion godhead Grace Jones and R&B songbird Aaliyah (respectively) as literal queens and figurative goddesses fallen to walk among the

mortals, able to captivate men with far more ease than when the gender dynamic is reversed.

They radiate raw eroticism; Jones' character Queen Katrina has even made a career out of it, appearing in the film as a dancer at an unnamed club. In the film's most bravura sequence, Queen Katrina does a serpentine, entrancing striptease routine to the main theme (which the real Jones also sings) for *Vamp*'s libidinous teen heroes. She unveils her body gradually, each new inch of skin revealing a Keith Haring-designed pattern painted all over, positing her as a living work of art. A deleted scene from *Queen of the Damned* saw Aaliyah in a similarly vaunted position, commanding the crowd with a single turn of her hips or dart of the eyes. Aaliyah's may be the vampire most in touch with her royal origins, in fact, seen fully decked out in a ceremonial bejeweled crown-necklace-top ensemble. Both films tremble before their women as sacred objects, their sexual fervor bordering on the religious.

And yet they're just that—objects. Both women are permitted to occupy inexplicably little space in what would ostensibly be their starring vehicles. (Of course, both films placed their sexy leading ladies front and centre in their advertising campaigns.) Aaliyah appears for approximately nineteen minutes in *Queen of the Damned's* 101-minute run time, a good portion of which is taken up by a leering, inelegant sex scene. Jones doesn't fare much better. Her character is entirely mute, communicating with the occasional look, but more often spoken for by others. Her appearance reinforces this nonhuman nature, Jones' skin caked with ghost-white pancake make-up that freezes her thousand-yard model stare in a mask verging on abstract. For characters of limitless power, they have suspiciously little agency and their presence tends to orient itself around someone else's story, that someone usually being a man. They're given short shrift twice over, first as black, then as black women.

Aaliyah and Jones embody one specific pocket of a much wider and more intricate politics of feminine representation in the canon of vampire cinema. While the camera's tug-of-war between awe and lasciviousness join these two women of colour with a larger body of work, other female vampires have brought the narrative tradition down daring, difficult new avenues. Hell hath no fury, it would appear, like a woman undead.

CHAPTER
SIX

THE
FEMALE
VAMPIRE

Vampirus
Vampira

Historically speaking, men have proven exceptionally skilled at making women into monsters. Sowing suspicion through superstition has been a valuable tool for securing and reinforcing the hegemonic status quo, and male insecurity can beget some frightful creatures. Ancient mythologies warn of succubi, demons assuming a pleasing feminine shape to tempt men into sexual congress and siphon their life force right out, genitals-first. The "witch hunts" that swept Europe and visited the Massachusetts Bay colony funneled rebellion against puritanical repression into hatred for women who failed to adhere to the community's strict standards of conduct. And as a beast woven from free-floating worry over decay, parasitism, sexuality, and temptation, the vampire was a ready-made way to demonize ambitious, unruly women.

The vampire is the traditional femme fatale with a supernatural bite, amplifying the erotic pull of Dracula and his acolytes, sometimes infusing it with a subversive edge in the process. Much like the black vampire, the female vampire began as a bad dream of the parties in power, then gradually reclaimed its own agency as attitudes glacially moved towards progressivism. The evolution of the female vampire corresponds to the long, hard-won march of feminism into the mainstream. When the social revolutions of the '60s and '70s took hold, the female vampire learned to wield its own terrible power and reshape its persona for hair-raising cautionary tales.

Starting with the title, 1936's *Dracula's Daughter* presents womanhood only insofar as it relates to maleness. Audiences of the era considered the film's total absence of Lugosi to be a short con and left it to wither in theaters, but stand-in Countess Marya Zaleska (Gloria Holden) amounts to a serviceable substitute. Fittingly, she spends the film struggling to get out of the penumbra cast by her father's legacy. Director Lambert Hillyer begins with Zaleska burning Dracula's remains in an effort to rid herself of her vampiric curse, the first in a series of oppositional gestures levied against the male authority figures in her life. Hillyer superimposed multiple archetypes of masculine panic onto Zaleska: she plays the "hysterical woman" when she shows herself to be beyond psychiatric help, and the strong homoerotic undertones ("Save the Women of London from Dracula's Daughter," went the poster's tagline) position her as a threat to male exclusivity over female bodies.

But the psychological torment and faint whiffs of lesbianism are the very pegs upon which current feminist reappraisals can be mounted. Determined scholars won't let authorial intention get in the way of appropriating Zaleska and her many daughters to reframe them as centres of tragedy and triumph. If Zaleska inspires fear in those around her, couldn't that be more a function of male frailty than her own intrinsic hideousness? In the real world, has stifled queer desire not been sublimated into ruinous dysfunction, sometimes even violence? She's a casualty of her own story, not a villain. As with the concubines headlining in 1960's *The Brides of Dracula* or the sapphic seductress Carmilla featured in 1960's *Blood and Roses* and 1970's *The Vampire Lovers*, she is too self-possessed for men to allow her to live, or at least live unperturbed.

Even the purview of the explicitly pornographic was malleable enough to invite feminist re-interpretation. Incorrigible Spanish horndog Jesús Franco didn't have goals much headier than getting his blood pumping when he made the disreputable, self-evidently named classics *Vampyros Lesbos* (1971) and *Female Vampire* (1975). Both films aspire to surface-level pleasures, primarily those of X-rated flesh and experiments with psychedelic color. The bloodsucking sirens of José Ramón Larraz's 1974 exploitation gem *Vampyres* were also contrived as male playthings, trapped in a vampire porno more "porno" than "vampire."

Their contemporary Jean Rollin brought a touch more avant-garde artistry to his sojourns through the wilds of vampire erotica. His most critically vaunted films—*The Nude Vampire* in 1970, *The Shiver of the Vampires* and *Requiem for a Vampire* in 1971—bask in the glow of their ripely sexual subjects, all the while smuggling in jarring formal and narrative deviations. Rollin concocts cockamamie narratives and abandons them when he loses interest; floods moonlit midnight cemetery ceremonies with luminescent reds and blues; plays a death-by-nipple-tassel scene with his tongue only half in cheek. These directors didn't directly encode challenging political content into their films, and yet even an image as immutable as a woman grinding her pudenda against a bedpost can be wrested from its critical context and nobly warped in a feminist analysis.

Along with Harry Kümel's 1971 film *Daughters of Darkness*, Franco and Rollin's films were originally conceived through the objectifying "male

gaze" of a peeping camera, fodder for masturbators with somewhat more open-minded tastes. But their presentations of unabashed female pleasure have a value beyond titillation. Some women in the present day have come to appreciate the over-the-top sexuality for its camp value, and developed a certain affinity for the exaggerated male estimate of a woman's inner erotic workings. Anna Biller's 2016 fever dream *The Love Witch* focuses on a separate supernatural terrain, but her affectionate nods to the vintage pulp cheapies that inspire her illustrates this principle all the same. So *Vampyros Lesbos* may not have been designed with real live lesbians in mind. Regardless, it radiates sexual heat so strongly that its go-for-broke randy spectacle still manages an entertainment value between detached bemusement and a turn-on.

Around the same time that feminist media criticism began picking apart and reassembling female-vampire films born misogynist, cinema learned how to do it for them. The genre matured as filmmakers gave their subjects motivations and goals more internally contained; self-actualization on an eternal scale eclipsed the single-minded pursuit of a man's (or woman's) love. The female vampire was allowed to tackle the great existential concerns that her Y-chromosome counterparts had been wrestling with for years, and the universal components of womanhood—learning familiarity with blood, being thought of as unknowable by men—only bolstered the themes of alienation coursing through the vampire canon. The sexual themes outgrew their hormonal obviousness as well, interrogating the desire impulse with more psychological nuance. At times, sex is a method of placating a gnawing emptiness, and at others, it's a low-grade form of self-destruction. Coming-of-age narratives for young women use sex to simultaneously empower and imperil, and while the vampiric slant on that paradox made for a foolproof schematic for success in porn, more empathetic dramas would use it to coax out higher emotional truths.

Tony Scott's 1983 ne plus ultra female vampire film *The Hunger* laid a lot of the groundwork for *Only Lovers Left Alive*. Indeed, Miriam Blaylock—the temptress portrayed by Catherine Deneuve, so smooth and spotless she could have been cut from marble—is cool in the same respect that Jarmusch's Adam and Eve are cool. She dresses impeccably, at once indivisible from the industrial-goth style of the '80s, steeped in a collage of styles from the past, and ahead of her time. An early, oft-cited scene follows Miriam and her David Bowie-played lover John—and could there possibly be anything in life cooler than dating David Bowie?—into an NYC discotheque where they entice their prey to come home with them under the implied guise of a group sexual dervish. Miriam and John appear to us first as punk-bohemian-libertines both for their advanced sexual tastes and flawless choices in finery, Deneuve breathtaking in cat-eye sunglasses and a military-styled fascinator.

through this love-'em-and-leave-'em cycle dozens of times over, her compartmentalization visualized in the scores of coffins containing her exes' howling remains that she stashes in her attic. This callous routine revitalizes Miriam in proportion with its sapping of others, and in the film's objectionably tidy climax, vice versa. She's a malevolent, predatory figure, but Scott grants her a grain of humanity by showing that she does this because she must rather than can, and that she feels the sting of regret.

In the grander scheme of her gender, Miriam's inaccessibility makes sense as a pre-emptive defense strategy. From Medea to Lisbeth Salander, fiction is littered with women who build walls around themselves after repeated negative experiences with men instill a learned suspicion instinct. Miriam insulates herself from the injuries of heartbreak by striking first, and Scott's interested in showing what happens when she selects someone too prepared to be ensnared. Of course Miriam would meet her match in another woman — Sarandon's degenerative cell researcher Sarah has the foundation in medical esoterica to get the drop on Miriam, but one gets the sense she sees her on a deeper level as well.

The intuitive kinship between Miriam and Sarah, as women and as patients of the vampiric germ, makes their attraction intense but untenable. The second Miriam and Sarah make eye contact, the synapse-busting sex they're going to have is inevitable. When Miriam makes an early overture of flirtation to Sarah, she responds, "Are you making a pass at me, Ms. Blaylock?" The phrase states resistance to the advance, but its playful wording and low-key nod to *The Graduate*'s famed seduction scene (at thousands of years old, Miriam is the queen of all cougars) invite Miriam closer. When their pent-up tension finally combusts in a gauzy sex scene, the screen runs the risk of bursting into flames. Their shared sensation of rightness, of this being their destiny, activates Miriam's fight-and-flight instinct and seals Sarah's doom. Until, that is, Sarah submits to the same urge to push away.

Miriam makes herself an island in the name of preservation, and for it, incurs a fatal punishment from the authorial powers that be. The female vampire's self-sufficiency intimidates existing male power structures even before she begins leeching directly from them to gain their power. Like so many of her undead sisters, she's partially in the wrong and partially wronged, driven to regrettable extremes but only in response to things that happen to her. Contradictions like this are hardwired into a woman's life: sexuality is desired then shamed, beauty is prized then feared, independence is demanded then reprimanded. It's a losing game, and the film finds Miriam notable for growing cold enough to last more rounds than anyone else.

Irrespective of whether their hearts continue to beat, women simply can't catch a break. Even those vampires willing to embrace the full sum of their savagery in an effort to tame it run the risk

of being overtaken. Claire Denis cross-breeds the temptress archetype with the feral vampire for her opaque 2001 film *Trouble Every Day*, sealing them both within the fetching figure of French screen idol Béatrice Dalle. As Coré, the mononym upping her overall feminine mystique, she ravages men with such wanton aggression that her husband must keep her contained in locked quarantine while he goes about his daily work. The image of a man literally placing a woman in bondage would seem to make Denis' point leadenly clear, but she's got a more finely shaded appraisal of womanhood in mind. Coré's husband hides her away for her own good, knowing that the trail of corpses she leaves in her wake would attract unfriendly attention if left unchecked. As he goes about the drudgery of burying the men she mutilates, an unanticipated devotional streak emerges. Denis doesn't mean to chide Coré or her man, instead forlornly shaking her head at the bitter curse of a woman's might, too much even for her to bear.

The most recent advance of this filmic lineage came from Neil Jordan's 2013 marvelous chamber piece *Byzantium*, which had the bright idea of tapping Saoirse Ronan and Gemma Arterton to portray daughter and mother vampires, respectively. The uncommon film to give a female vampire a counterpart to play off, it granted the two women a sense of sisterhood that didn't have to be sullied by the lewd demands of softcore. Their Gothic-roustabout lifestyle of roving from town to town demands at least a minimum of solidarity, with each woman leaping to the other's aid in their most dire moments. They're prone to play games and bicker and freeze one another out like any other parent-child pairing, but their unenviable circumstances deepen their bond to a rarefied level.

Being a film about female vampires, of course, the question of desire figures prominently in the story, linking the present-day and historical halves of the century-jumping plot. But Jordan places lust under a larger umbrella of love, which he frames from a more circumspect vantage point than most. Both women share a platonic love vulcanized by time and blood, cemented over hundreds of years in a trust no man could ever violate. Even so, high on her permanent teenage hormones, Ronan falls into the whirlwind of adolescent infatuation with a local boy. She wants love in an uncompromised state, and so she attempts to diminish the influence of her vampirism through ethics, feeding only on the willing. This is easier said than done.

There's a precious treasure waiting at the conclusion of *Byzantium*, for those willing to crawl through the mile of blood that leads there: a happy ending. Jordan lets his women make it out alive (relatively speaking) and with the apples of their eyes safely in tow, an ordinary wrap-up notable only in its divergence from the doctrine of tragedy applied to female vampire writing. Comeuppances both deserved and not-so always befall the women touched by the vampiric germ, blanketing the subgenre with a woe that almost draws annoyance when considered on a big-picture scale. A curious party might start to wonder where the fun female vampire movies are hiding. Just as queer audiences have cried out for non-hetero films unburdened by po-faced pain, the female vampire seemingly can't cast a furtive glance in some pretty thing's direction without marking herself for a fall. This starts to explain the weird dearth of a female Dracula, a populist favourite character capable of enduring for multiple installments over time; art primarily understands womanhood, and usually rightly so, as a site for catastrophe. As in the human plane, saddled with a responsibility that she was born into and never asked for, the female vampire soldiers on. She's looking for a hot meal; whether that's euphemistic or not varies.

CHAPTER
SEVEN

THE
WESTERN
VAMPIRE

Vampirus
Varminticus

The vampire is homeless in America, a stranger in a strange land. The creature's history is that of outsiderdom—of being a monster among humans, ageless among the aging, a foreigner in the States. Dracula's Transylvanian breeding makes this disconnect literal, but his intrinsic European roots cast deeper and more significant influence on the character's makeup. It's not incidental that Dracula's a Count, a remnant of a feudal ruling system long since fallen into obsolescence. He radiates an air of superiority, both as an advanced predatory organism and as a ruler among subjects. His regal composure dates him even as it provides the basis for his powers of persuasion, granting him command of the world while he sequesters himself from it. He's a loner. Dracula doesn't have cohorts, never mind friends. He has minions.

His status as a frequent outcast extends to genre as well, another cultural gate he had to pass through in bat-form under the cover of night. Theoretically, there should be no place for Dracula and his kind in cinema's first truly American narrative tradition, the Western. On even the most rudimentary conceptual levels, vampire lore doesn't sync up with the genre's value system and thematic preoccupations. The

Western canon tells the sprawling origin story of a patchwork nation, observing how shared principles help disparate collections of people knit the chaos of nature into the order of society. In the clear-cut ethical showdown between the valiant cowboy defender and the no-goodniks threatening town—a Manichean struggle between good and evil—the vampire occupies an uncomfortable middle ground. These questions of agreed-upon societal pacts mean nothing to the vampire. The Western specifically examines the vital utility of laws; the vampire has no use for such petty regulations. They're immaterial to him, ignored rather than broken. When a vampire feeds, he's heeding nature's most basic call. Laws have no place in a matter this visceral.

But just as Dracula's popularity mandated that Abbot and Costello awkwardly integrate him into their dimension of antic comedy, so too did the vampire inevitably set a track for the frontier. And in William Beaudine's unimaginatively-named *Billy the Kid vs. Dracula*, the pairing of subject and narrative mode was equally incongruous, integrating the character on only the most superficial level. As the title suggests, the 1966 film sees Dracula (played here by John Carradine, continuing on with the character after succeeding Bela Lugosi in

Universal's films) arriving in an Old West town in search of—what else—a suitable bride. He sets his sights on the ripest peach in the settlement, who just so happens to be betrothed to the famed gunslinger. The terms of their conflict, then, are not ideological but romantic. The central friction of the Western comes from the doctrine of supremacy through brutish domination—Hobbes' hypothesized state of nature—grinding against the impulse to attain a higher standard of living through civility. This film reduces that complex battle to a glorified todger-measuring contest in which one contestant also possesses superpowers.

Everything about the film was slapdash; shot in eight days and paid for by then-independent outfit Embassy Pictures with pocket change, Carradine openly considered it the worst film he ever appeared in. That was not the first time the vampire followed Lewis and Clark's path through the great plains, however. Seven years before Dracula descended on the Corriganville Movie Ranch, Universal made the bold decision to pursue a vampire film that would not fall in line with the mythology of their Lugosi-fronted properties, or even attempt to capitalize on the blooming popularity of Hammer's pictures. During the late 1950s, writing partners and spouses Edward

and Mildred Dein shared a running off-colour joke about an idea for "a Western horror story about a fag vampire running around the desert eating little boys." Word eventually got back to Universal producer Joseph Gershenson, who challenged the pair to put their money where their mouths were. Hardly the first Hollywood picture born of a joke taken seriously, it would not be the last.

The Deins initially wrote *Curse of the Undead* as a satire, and in a move critics describe as "the reverse Dr. Strangelove," the script dissolved into a more straight-faced suspense picture during production. All the same, the motivating spark remained unaltered — this film digs its fangs a little deeper into the mishmash notion of the Western vampire than most, carving out a little space in town for him to occupy as opposed to sticking him in wherever spot's easiest, however ill-fitting. By starting from square one with a character who has had sufficient opportunity to integrate himself into his surroundings, the film finds him a place not just in the fabric of his own film, but the more vast moral dimension that informs the Western.

Mixing the archetype of the usual oater baddie—a rival pistol jockey, identifiable by his black hat and bad attitude—with the vampire could've been simple enough for the Deins. They go the extra mile by integrating the Western's guiding sense of piety tied up in Christian dogma into the biology, background and fate of Michael Pate's so-called "Drake Robey." A mysterious wanderer intervening in the feud between neighboring ranchers, Robey conducts himself with the same laughable obviousness that outed his forebears as something other than human. (Choice line: when a local asks Robey if he feels any trepidation about living next to a graveyard, he positively purrs, "The dead don't bother me, it's the living that cause me trouble.")

He's hiding more than his species—the film whips Robey's origin out of its proverbial sleeve at the denouement, exposing him as Drago Robles, son of the Spanish nobleman who founded the contested ranch decades earlier. A preserved diary tells of Drago returning to the ranch from a Spanish sojourn to find his wife has shacked up with his brother, spurring him to stab his traitorous sibling before turning the dagger on himself out of sheer anguish. His vampirism takes hold spontaneously following his suicide (a holdover from a European superstition

But in America, who does? A nation of immigrants, founded on genocide and rising to superpower status through slavery and imperialism, the United States is young enough to have been continually writing and rewriting its own history since its inception. In no channel of pop culture is the shifting tide of American self-opinion more clearly apparent than the Western as the '50s hit and the genre changed course from nationalist myth-making to puncturing deconstruction. Early Westerns vaunted cowboys as broad-shouldered defenders of the defenceless, standing for all that was right and good in the savage wild-lands of the unsettled frontier. Mustache-twirling, spur-jangling villains would take pool hall damsels hostage, and the gallant cow-puncher would stride into town, pistols at dawn, all's well that ends well. Ever the arbiter of prairie Americana, John Ford submitted young lawyer/President-to-be Abraham Lincoln as the uber-cowboy in 1939's *Young Mr. Lincoln*, enforcing harmony not through the gun but with the letter of the law. By 1956's *The Searchers*, Ford had replaced him with John Wayne's Ethan Edwards, a cantankerous and racist old man getting left behind by his time. A starkly different mold of "hero," he painted a decidedly less flattering portrait

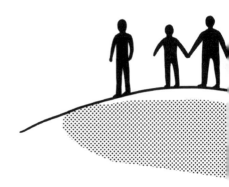

of early America as a land forged through bigotry and brutality.

With the 1987 ramble *Near Dark*, Kathryn Bigelow picked up the neo-Western's introspective mantle and used the vampire to drive the subgenre to arid existential flatlands. The roving band of varmints—never referred to as vampires by name, as if they're any other pack of drifters—that snap unsuspecting freshly-minted vampire Caleb (Adrian Pasdar) up into their ranks follow the same wandering star as the cowboy and the bandit archetypes. They all share a placelessness, bouncing between locations they cannot hope to make their home. *The Searchers* ends with the totemic image of Ethan standing before a doorway, a threshold the vampire likewise cannot cross.

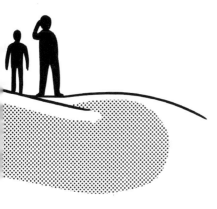

The colourful retinue of bloodsuckers—
including Bill Paxton as a wackadoo sadist who says
things like "Howdy, I'm gonna separate yer head
from yer shoulders, hope you don't mind none,"
and a chain-smoking child who's actually hundreds
of years old—chase their appetite from settlement
to settlement, leaving a bloody path of massacres
behind them. Natural enemies of the sun that beats
down with extreme prejudice on the sleepy towns
dotting the modern West, the vampires feel secure
only when in their light-tight RV. Credit Bigelow
and co-writer Eric Red with investing more thought
than most into the logistics of being a vampire while
mobile. (A scene in which the vampires frantically
duct-tape over their windows, dodging slivers of light
like lasers, is one of the film's most unexpectedly

gripping.) They live by night, scurrying away from the dawn like cockroaches; as lovelorn Mae (Jenny Wright) finds when she takes a likin' to Caleb, it's a lonely lot.

As the two of them sit under a constellation-strewn sky, Mae dispenses a bit of home-on-the-range poetry: "The light that's leaving that star right now will take a billion years to get down here. You want to know why you've never met a girl like me before?" she asks Caleb. "Because I'll still be here when the light from that star gets down here to earth in a billion years." Roving across the plains closely acquaints the cowboy with isolation, and while the Westerns of yore got sentimental about solitude as a virtue—consider the romanticized perspectives on "the strong, silent type" and the vast unpeopled expanses of nature's splendor—later reappraisals would see in it a restless searching impulse instead. The vampires' hunt for meat is more material than spiritual, but the Sisyphean aspect of their insatiable hunger aligns them with the indefinitely wandering cowboy and his pursuant bandit.

The Western affirms that loneliness is a necessity for survival in a climate where life can be taken in a fraction of a second, which *Near Dark* echoes with its own gratuitous violence. The dangers inseparable from the vampire's pattern of feeding and travelling make close interpersonal relationships with humans untenable, and only when Mae and Caleb revert to human form (via rather convenient blood transfusions) can they begin their romance in earnest. The cowboy nobly sacrifices romance much like the superhero, knowing that close links could imperil their loved ones and be exploited as a vulnerability. In *Near Dark*, Mae and Caleb repeatedly rejigger their DNA to avoid this hazard: with a single bite, she turns him undead and jumps the boy into her crew, only for Caleb to return to his human roots upon accepting that he doesn't have the gumption to kill (in the film's most disarmingly tender moment, Mae feeds Caleb from an open bite on her own arm when he cannot bring himself to sink his own fangs), after which Mae joins him on the side of the living. Bigelow poses brash challenges to the established tropes of Western storytelling, and where she sees fit, freely flips the script.

Through the vampire, Bigelow cut right to the soul of the Western; in his 1996 genre crossover *From Dusk till Dawn*, Robert Rodriguez merely adopted the genre's finery and structure. The Quentin Tarantino-scripted horror-comedy plops a family and the pair of petty crooks holding them at gunpoint in a sleazy Mexican strip joint, where all the patrons and dancers — including and especially the magnificently-named Santanico Pandemonium, portrayed by Salma Hayek from the proud example of *Vamp*'s Grace Jones—also happen to be vampires. Though the film appends a classically Fordian redemptive ending to principled bandit Seth Gecko (a handsome young cad named George Clooney), it borrows the aesthetics of the Western and the vampire without its attendant ideas. All the

standoffs are necessarily Mexican, and the setting gives Rodriguez the chance to indulge his penchant for minute detail in set-dressing. But Rodriguez follows a schematic beginning with *Rio Bravo* and continuing right on through to John Carpenter's 1998 film *Vampires*. He strands his characters, and leaves them to fight their way out through hordes of faceless enemies.

Though demonstrably dumber under every conceivable vector of criticism, at least the film's direct-to-video spawn, sequel *Texas Blood Money*

and prequel *The Hangman's Daughter*, take the franchise a little closer to its cultural roots. The third installment, which joins a new ensemble of characters in Mexico during the early 20th century, glancingly examines the role Mexico played in the rocky settlement of the American West with a pair of Christian missionaries intruding on the country while Pancho Villa's revolutionary armies run amok. Though Rodriguez and his journeyman successors never seemed all that dedicated to the idea in the first place, these films never fully integrate the vampire into the milieu of the Western. They share a screen, but never meld to fill it.

The speedy decline of Rodriguez's rinky-dink empire cannily illustrates the hazards of imposing vampirism on a mismatched narrative body. The Western vampire would seem an unlikely hybrid, born perhaps out of visions of dollar signs but ultimately rising to justify its own existence. Though the world continues to await patiently the first vampire legal thriller, the broad, enduring appeal of the creature would get him unnaturally fused with all manner of genres and styles over the years, and one permutation was more counterintuitive than all the rest. The vampire had gone West, gone pornographic, even gone to space. (Though the creatures in Mario Bava's sci-fi gem *Planet of the Vampires* are really closer to zombies.) The truest final frontier for these undead predators subsisting on warm mammal blood was a PG rating. Vampires: you know, for kids!

THE CHILDISH VAMPIRE

Vampirus Juvenalius

n 1945, Japan's national character had arrived at a crossroads. The Allied forces' atomic bombing of Nagasaki and Hiroshima had ended World War II with an unconditional surrender that left the Japanese population in a crisis of confidence. The country had been made an example of, totally demilitarized with the addition of the Japanese Constitution's Article 9 and stripped of the estimable power it previously wielded. While the unease about a scientifically engineered annihilation would go on to give us Godzilla, this same undercurrent of postwar anxiety would seed a more telling cultural phenomenon as well.

Osamu Tezuka created the Astro Boy character in 1952, an entire arsenal's worth of firepower in the unassuming package of a pint-size youngster. He provides one of the earliest examples in a rich bloodline of Japanese art centered around characters possessing great strength that's not immediately, outwardly apparent. Some of the most widely recognized figures from their pop-culture banks— superpowered schoolgirl Sailor Moon, the many extraordinary critters of Pokémon, irrepressibly upbeat Hello Kitty, and a certain Tezuka creation dubbed Don Dracula—speak covertly to the national ideal of force hidden beneath a cutesy exterior. They even assigned a slang term to the to the state of being little and cute: *chibi*.

Beyond the limits of Japan, the vampire has been subject to a similarly curious cultural alchemy. It is the ultimate fate of everything in the universe to be eventually rendered as an adorable version of itself, most likely via the fawning legions of online fan-artists, but in some higher-profile cases, this happens in a more officially sanctioned capacity. In its dogged pursuit of every conceivable twist on the vampire legend, cinema has sporadically explored the juxtaposition of the creature's core traits—a set that varies, but always includes the hunger for blood and exception from death—with a kinder, gentler demeanor. Some films have kneeled down to meet the child's eye-level, others have looked back from a taller perspective, and the best among them locate a primal common ground between the turbulence of youth and the vampire's barely-controllable urges.

A fair number of kiddie-geared entertainments have chibi-fied their vampires for the sake of family-friendliness, altering the character only by sanding off his edges. Scores of small-screen programs go this safely paved route, more so than at the multiplex. (It's anyone's guess why that is; I suspect it has something to do with movies relying more heavily on a familiarity with vampire iconography that school-age viewers have not yet established, while TV charges a lower mental price of admission.) Characters like *Sesame Street*'s Count von Count are blunt objects, usually styled after Lugosi's Dracula, and scrubbed of the integral vampiric qualities that extend beyond the visual. To an unwitting toddler, the Count's no more than a purple-skinned puppet with a widow's peak and a funny voice.

In its truest incarnation, the vampire is inappropriate for pre-teen audiences in both the typical schoolmarm meaning and a deeper thematic undertow. Kids frighten easy, and conveying an overall mood of spookiness without scaring the pudding out of them requires a delicate balancing act. But more to the point, the vampire's essence being tangled in sex and death would render it unrecognizable on a spiritual level to children. The vampire's symbolic mechanisms make no sense to someone who has not yet reached the age where a mind can conceive of mortality and desire. Which is what makes *Hotel Transylvania* such a miraculous motion picture.

The bright, primary-colour-happy animation style clearly identifies Genndy Tartakovsky's 2012 feature as safe territory even before the PG rating can. It's a kids' movie through and through, but like

the director's superlative sci-fi TV series *Samurai Jack*, the film has been invested with a unobtrusive maturity. Tartakovsky stays true to many of the most steadfast through-lines in the vampire canon, including lust, loss, and most particularly, isolation.

The film begins with a bruising death and reactive retreat: Dracula (Adam Sandler, doing his Adam Sandlerest funny-voice) builds the grand hotel of the title following his wife's murder at the hands of an angry mob of humans. What might be the happy ending to a different film is here a sad beginning, spurring him to seal himself and his prized daughter Mavis away from the human world in a refuge for monsters of all sorts. Fear remains a key component of the vampire's personal makeup, but Drac's now on the receiving end. He can bug his face out all spooky when he wants to, but the mere presence of a human being in his hotel sets him into finger-fluttering worry for himself and his daughter. Losing his wife toughens him into an overprotective parent, an unfamiliar role for the vampire to play.

Of course, the parents in the audience immediately recognize the impulse to shelter, alien as it may be to the vampire's legacy. One of the minor challenges faced by children's entertainment is playing to both the youth faction of the viewership as well as the put-upon adults who have dragged them to the multiplex, given corporeal form here in avatar Drac. As in Pixar's fishy *Searchers* riff *Finding Nemo*, his skittishness exemplifies the pressures of parenthood, another experience largely unknown to the vampire; when creating new spawn, the vampire usually assumes a romantic relationship with its charge, and a mentor-mentee dynamic barring that.

Though Drac acts like an inveterate goofball, the truly childish vampire is Mavis, and her arc provides children with a workable primer to the confusing, irrational experiences that await them in puberty. The vampire's foundation of sex and death first makes itself known in adolescence, and childish vampires like Mavis put those intimidating galaxies of knowledge into more simply digestible terms.

Mavis fosters the same pupil-dilating hunger that motivates an adult vampire, replacing the need for flesh with a more generalized lust for life. Like so many young people, she's itching to get out and broaden her horizons, as constrained within her daddy's fortress as any small-town tween might feel in their suburb. When a human backpacker unknowingly wanders into the Hotel Transylvania in search of a bed for the night, Mavis immediately sees in him a taste of the outside world. And in a kid-sanctioned device, Tartakovsky funnels her yearning for life beyond her father's walls back into the vampire's signature erotic charge; when Mavis and her mate first lock eyes, they're both seized by a sudden wave of arousal known as "the Zing." In a musical number closing out the film, lyrics define the Zing as an emotional occurrence, that unmistakable love-at-first-sight feeling that informs the lonesome that they've found their one true amour. As a knee-jerk bodily response, however, savvier viewers recognize the Zing as something not too far removed from an erection of the heart.

Tartakovsky splits a lot of differences, proving his mastery by avoiding any awkwardness in his contrasts: Drac's cuddly but menacing when he wants to be, Mavis' tentative courtship is chaste and yet hormonally roiling just below the liminal register, mature elements are present and yet not fully interrogated. The film sketches Drac and Mavis with broad strokes, setting up an analogous connection between the impulse-driven behavior of the child and the vampire without fully enmeshing the two. Films like *Hotel Transylvania* and *The Little Vampire* (Uli Edel's 2000 adaptation of a German novel series of the same name) work in half-measures, providing an easy

Tomas Alfredson's superb *Let the Right One In* shuffles down the same path as *The Little Vampire*, assigning a friendless young boy a reserved undead playmate. Likewise, they bond as outcasts, and likewise, the vampire dispatches the human's bullies as a twisted token of affection. But just as Alfredson trades the rolling greens of Scotland for the barren, featureless snowfields of Sweden, so too does Edel's facile appraisal of the childish vampire give way to a far colder assessment of the type. By abandoning the sanitized, sugar-rush tone endemic to kiddie amusements, Alfredson is able to assemble a more truthful meditation on the tribulations of being a kid. Your 8-year-old probably wouldn't enjoy a film so sedate (or so violent), but the emotional mechanisms on screen would at least make sense to them.

In the seemingly endless winter of 1981, fragile Oskar moves to the Stockholm suburb of Blackburg with his single mother. He's already known dull throbs of hurt in his life, as we learn from an early scene in which Oskar's deadbeat dad ditches a night of father-son camaraderie to drink himself into a stupor with a friend. And as the morose new kid at school, it's a given that he'd attract some bullies— the lamentable lot of the lovable loser. When moppet vampire Eli enters his life, Oskar doesn't give a second thought to her withdrawn demeanor or pallid complexion. He's grateful for a lifeline. "I'm not a girl," goes the warning when Oskar tentatively asks Eli if she'd like to be his girlfriend. "I don't care," he responds. This exchange encapsulates their chemistry in miniature: knowing the danger she would bring upon him, Eli tries to push Oskar away, but they'd both rather

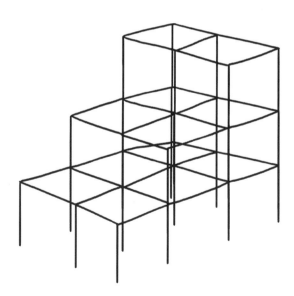

court peril together than trudge through their pre-pubescent years separately.

Though she cures Oskar of his loneliness and ultimately saves his life, Eli's far from the sort of writerly godsend to a sensitive boy that dots young-adult fiction. (Though she inspires Oskar to strike first against his most detested bully, she's not, one might say, a manic vampire dream girl.) Those in search of a comparison point would find one in Suzy of Wes Anderson's 2012 adventure film *Moonrise Kingdom*, an attractive presence and yet forbidding in her sudden jags of wanton rage and crushing sadness. Like her, the juvenile vampire qualifies as what pediatric psychiatrists of yore would've termed a "problem child," whose unruly, extreme feelings retard their psychosocial development and ostracize them from their peer group. In the more tolerantly-minded medical terminology of today, Eli would probably be described as "special needs." Indeed, her needs are quite special; she requires regular warm-blooded offerings, reluctantly but dutifully procured by her guardian Håkan.

Eli must provide for herself after Håkan sacrifices his body to feed her in a desperate situation, and it's then that the totality of the savagery contained within this compact package can break free. In one of Alfredson's most aesthetically satisfying shots, Eli leaps from above on a silhouetted figure framed by the arch of a tunnel. In the ensuing struggle, she ricochets off the curvature of the tunnel like a pinball, vast reservoirs of energy compressed into four and a half feet. Alfredson underscores this contrast most dramatically in the climactic massacre at the town pool, and he doesn't even have to show a thing. Alfredson sticks the camera underwater with an unconscious Oskar while Eli goes about slicing and dicing his tormentors, plopping severed limbs into the water silently, out of focus, and in the background. The sight that greets Oskar when he regains consciousness—Eli, covered into coagulated blood but with the slight smile of an innocent—epitomizes the warring swells of emotion in the mercurial childish vampire: prone to temper tantrums that leave a casualty count, and yet not fully estranged from the softness that adults prize in their offspring.

When director Matt Reeves announced in 2008 that he had signed on for an American remake to be titled *Let Me In*, he clarified that he intended to adapt the original novel, and not Alfredson's film. Be that as it may, his 2010 release borrowed liberally from Alfredson's playbook, even nicking some key shots from the Swedish version. Though Reeves added a begins to explain why the childish vampire, a creation that should work at cross purposes with itself at every conceptual turn, continues to resonate with viewers of all ages. Toddlers and school-agers spend formative years testing limits, figuring out what can and can't be done, eventually working their way to should and shouldn't. The childish vampire discovers that it has no such limits, and that the difference between could and should looks awfully immaterial from the perspective of an immortal.

It must be noted that the vampiric organism reaches sexual maturity far earlier than it reaches emotional maturity, resulting in some fascinating dissonances and patterns of dysfunctional relationships with humans. The primary symptom: skin that glitters in the sun like pretty, fancy diamonds.

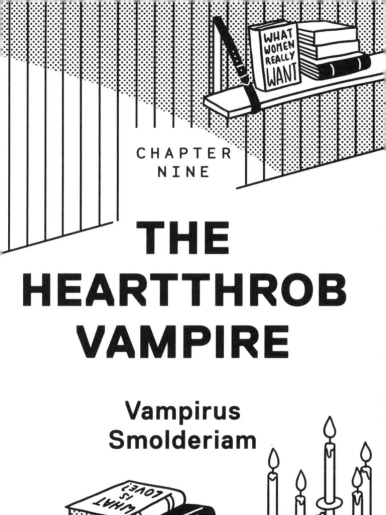

CHAPTER
NINE

THE HEARTTHROB VAMPIRE

Vampirus Smolderiam

In the early stages of planning for this book, I conducted some informal research among friends and colleagues to gauge which films would be of particular public interest. And every single person canvassed—young and old, male and female, highbrow and low—asked some variation of the same question. Some asked earnestly, some with detached ironic bemusement, some with a distant note of terror. But everyone wanted to be sure: "You're going to cover *Twilight*, right?"

Just as the Beatles were bigger than Jesus at the height of their popularity, another snazzy-haired dreamboat named Edward Cullen was at one point bigger than Dracula. There was a need in the US to replace the vacuum left by Harry Potter, which combined with the boy-band-boom generation's sexual coming-of-age for a juggernaut of almost maddening ubiquity. It claimed the teen-girl tastemaker as its patient zero in the late '00s before expanding to infect the mainstream through the cineplex. Stephenie Meyer's series of supernatural romance novels and the five film adaptations that followed have been credited with singlehandedly igniting a vampire craze that brought the creatures back into the monoculture's spotlight. TV attempted to piggyback with *True*

Blood and *The Vampire Diaries,* while Hollywood was so eager to leech some of *Twilight*'s popularity that it condoned such crimes against decency as *Abraham Lincoln: Vampire Hunter.* The vampire had never fully fallen out of fashion, and its rebranding for maximized youth appeal coincided with the perfect confluence of cultural factors.

But the T-shirts emblazoned with cheeky slogans pitting various "teams" against one another, the thousands upon thousands of tweenaged girls storming midnight premieres, and the untold volumes of fan-fiction spell out the essence of *Twilight*'s abnormal popularity in letters visible from space. The cause is bigger than its moment. Edward Cullen and his illegitimate progeny all exist for the playacting of romantic daydreams. (None more so than spanking enthusiast Christian Grey of *Twilight* fan-fiction *50 Shades of Grey,* though that's a different, at least triply insane kettle of fish.) Born as the idealized plaything of a bored housewife with steamy literary ambitions, Edward provides a receptacle for markedly girlish scenarios imbued with the glamor and swooning melodrama absent in its creator's everyday life. In this respect, though his mother may be Stephenie Meyer, Edward's grandmother is really Anne Rice.

Over a prolific career spanning 40-plus years, Rice has penned novels about mummies, witches, and the early childhood of Jesus Christ, and yet not even the Savior struck the same chord with readers as her most famed creation Lestat. The central character in her long-running Vampire Chronicles series of bodice-rippers (he pops up in *Queen of the Damned*, albeit in a more supporting capacity), he continues Dracula's legacy of bloodstained aristocracy, adding to it a genteel prettiness catering to the fanciful illusions shared between the author and her loyal readership. Rice fixates on minor details of Lestat's appearance like a seventh-grader staring at her crush in algebra class; we learn his eyes are gray but reflect blue and purple lights, which is both pretty and symbolic, while his fingernails appear to be made of spotless glass. He's delicate, in touch with his feminine side to complement his masculine vitality.

Lestat couldn't have found a more apt human vessel than Tom Cruise for Neil Jordan's 1994 film adaptation of the character's debut book, *Interview with the Vampire*. Blessed with a jaw that could cut diamond and outfitted with a wig full of golden, flowing tresses, Cruise pushed the debonair vampire archetype to its next evolutionary phase: the heartthrob. The film introduces Lestat with fitting pomp and circumstance, mentioned before he's seen to build the fog of intrigue. He draws on the same reserves of erotic magnetism that brought Dracula willing nubile necks, and softens it with a gentlemanly chivalry. He's a sex object for an era shedding its shyness about sex, when palpable expressions of desire were migrating inward from the exploitation periphery to more socially acceptable territory.

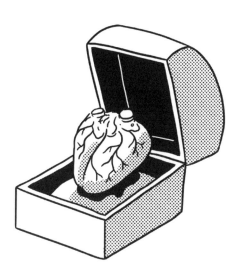

Cruise co-starred with Brad Pitt, perhaps the other most slobbered-over star of their moment, and the homoerotic sparks flying between them start to clarify the heartthrob vampire's inner workings. Pitt portrays Louis de Pointe du Lac, another well-to-do member of the landed gentry in ante-bellum New Orleans, and the victim of a chance encounter with the night stalker Lestat. Though "victim" doesn't fully cover it — Louis gives himself over willingly to Lestat when offered the option to become a vampire, having just lost his wife and child. Starting from the moment of conversion, a tableau of one man surrendering himself fully to the whims of the man whose lips are on his neck, the bond between them dangerously straddles the line between parental and sexual.

Lestat and Louis interact like mentor and mentee in some scenes, and like a May-December married couple in others. When Lestat playfully chides Louis for "whining" about the change he intended as a gift—chuckling "Louis, Louis, Louis" so smugly that only a star of Cruise's magnitude could pull it off—it's unclear whether we're supposed to hear this as a parent's reprimand or the affectionate scold of an older lover. Pitt and Cruise exchange no shortage of loaded looks, enough that a viewer can almost hear a crowd chanting "kiss, kiss, kiss" at a dull roar. Lestat takes inexperienced Louis under his wing and initiates him in the ways of the vampire, laying the gay subtext as bare as the time would allow. (In the novel, Lestat directly propositions Louis. Even in 1994, Jordan couldn't get away with that.) Their spousal dynamic even brings them a surrogate daughter in the form of Claudia (Kirsten Dunst), and after she and Louis turn on Lestat, he continues to stalk them as the most persistent abusive ex to have ever lived.

Lestat is all things to Louis: savior and tormentor, security and danger, soulmate and sworn enemy. The heartthrob vampire blends every hue of feeling together into a single sweaty fervor of overwhelming desire. Conventional wisdom states that hate and love are but two sides of the same coin; while Lestat and Louis' relationship sustains a high standard of intensity, whether it's positive or negative can reverse with one cross word. Their blood may run cold, but their tempers only run hot. And though Rice wrote the original text as an adult, about two men for whom age has faded into irrelevance, this mindset smacks of adolescence. In those awkward years between physical and emotional maturity, when the body

of libidinous hangups that is *Twilight*. Across four novels and five movies, Meyer's rigid set of personal principles chemically reacted with her complete lack of delicacy as a storyteller to form the most transparent display of naked (or rather, strategically-clothed) wish-fulfillment in modern literature. The tragedy of star-crossed lovers Bella Swan and Edward Cullen supplied Meyer with a receptacle for all of her most breathless fantasies, from the perfect meet-cute to a day-by-day breakdown of a dream wedding and picturesque honeymoon. Meyer set her novels in the cozy township of Forks, Washington, ostensibly because the constant cloud-cover suits the light-allergic vampires. Still, when the hefty *Twilight* cheques started rolling in, Meyer's first big-ticket purchase was a second home on Marrowstone Island in the Pacific Northwest. To an outside observer, it might look like she had taken one step closer to imitating her art with her life.

In Bella and Edward, she laid a blank canvas onto which she could scrawl not only an idealized vision of love, but of herself. As her name implies, Bella Swan (Kristen Stewart) epitomizes purity and preciousness; she's not like the popular girls, more comfortable eating a cheeseburger in her

Chuck Taylors than doing her make-up or hitting the mall. Nobody around town really understands her, neither her doting father (Billy Burke) nor the Veronica to Edward's Betty, her childhood bestie Jacob (Taylor Lautner). Most importantly, she's still a virgin, having kept her virtues untarnished by saving her "gift" for the right suitor. These vacancies waiting to be filled by a man contribute to an overall incompleteness, which seems to be the criterion by which Meyer judges Bella as an exemplar of womanhood. The author may be unimaginably wealthy, but she won't be earning special citations for feminist trailblazing any time soon.

Edward (Robert Pattinson), accordingly, enters Bella's life to provide her missing piece. As the heartthrob vampire, he's cut out to be everything she's ever wanted; he's absurdly handsome, from his gravity-defying shock of chestnut hair to his muscular-but-not-too-muscular physique. He commands the romantic attention of all the girls at their high school, yet he plays it aloof and never reciprocates their affections. A fabulously wealthy family and troubled past create the fog of mystery around him, an air only augmented by his vampirism, which takes him away from class for long, unexplained absences. His set of biological traits favors the heroic (super-speed, super-strength) and sidelines the monstrous (deformities, transformation into a bat).

Above all else, Edward loves Bella, unflaggingly and without limit. While the basis for their mutual attraction never really adds up, Edward would do anything for Bella from the moment he lays eyes on her. Like an emo Superman, Edward jumps to Bella's defence in the first film to crush a car sailing towards her, the first in a long series of protective gestures. He later takes his defensive instinct a step further and binds their souls for eternity so that whenever Bella's in danger, her subconscious sends a supernatural distress call. When she tells him at the close of final installment *Breaking Dawn Part 2* that "nobody's ever loved anybody as much as I love you," a thought that only a teenager could have, he grins and tells her that "there's one exception." Edward cares for Bella with a fanatical devotion none of us can hope to fathom — so much so that he refuses to have sex with her.

In the simplest possible terms, *Twilight* is an epic about one girl who wants to get laid so badly that she's willing to die to do it. Bella takes her first hits of oestrogen hard, and wastes no time putting the moves on Edward once they've struck up a proper relationship. In keeping with Meyer's tenet of Mormon abstinence, however, their genitals must remain pristine and untouched until holy matrimony. So Edward rebuffs Bella's advances and tells her that they cannot get physical so long as a barrier separates their species; though he puts the point in more tactful language, Edward explains to her that the force of vampiric lovemaking is such that a dalliance between them would leave her puny human body a smoldering sexual crater. "When we taste human blood, a frenzy sets in," Edward warns Bella in the first film. "We can't stop it." This is not altogether unwelcome; beyond undying commitment, Edward brings a sorely needed sense of danger into Bella's life. That he could purportedly blast her to smithereens with the sheer velocity of his penis frightens Bella, but the prospect of being the only woman able to soothe his savage breast is too much to be denied. Edward gives Bella more than love — he gives her entire life purpose.

Meyer later backtracks to contradict herself, and Edward agrees to deflower Bella as a human only if she first marries him and then willingly joins him in vampirism directly afterward. The sequence of events doesn't quite make sense in terms of the script's architecture or internal logic, but it falls squarely in line with Meyer's personally held convictions about piety. Both in Mormon orthodoxy and the typical teenage psychology, sex represents a daunting entry into the unknown. Feared and coveted in equal measure, the forbidden fruit (less-than-subtly encoded via an apple adorning the hardcover edition's jacket) drives Bella to troubling extremes that cut to the rotten core of the heartthrob vampire.

Meyer samples liberally from *Romeo and Juliet* for sophomore outing *New Moon*, feeding Edward lines of Shakespearean verse for him to recite to Bella. (The heartthrob vampire must balance brawn with brains; Edward attains the elusive lumberjack-scholar ideal.) Having set up the franchise's primary conflict as the feud between Edward's family and a cabal of elder vampires known as the Volturi, Meyer's drawing a baldfaced parallel with Shakespeare's tragedy, playing into the age-old misread of the play as suggesting that true love can conquer all to transcend trivial differences. She deals Edward and Bella the happily-ever-after that Romeo and Juliet never got, allowing them to spend eternity together on Earth instead of in their celestial resting place. But Meyer's worldview blinds her to Shakespeare's deeper warnings about the follies of acting rashly. Both pairs of teens sabotage themselves in the name of what they believe to be an adamantine love; Bella dies, though that's a minor price to pay when immortality awaits her. More to the point, she abandons all her friends and her family to sign the rest of forever away to a man she met earlier that year. Meyer finds this all quite romantic; read between the lines, and a more problematic portrait of mutually supportive love emerges.

ASSORTED SPECIMENS FROM AROUND THE GLOBE

There are, by anybody's count, a lot of vampire movies. A broad survey of the genre suggests that hundreds upon hundreds of features contain a vampiric character or some element of vampirism. Organizing them into categories along thematic and aesthetic criteria has helped to cover a lot of ground, but there are simply too many vampire films worth watching to collect in a guide such as this without expanding to an unwieldy size. As a last-ditch attempt to cover all bases in need of covering, included here are ten more outstanding titles hailing from ten different national film economies. Safe travels.

Korea — *Thirst*

South Korea's Park Chan-wook has achieved international recognition in part due to his ability to expropriate Western genres and exert his *sui generis* influence over them to create something partially recognizable while at once demonstrably new. Park turned again to Europe for inspiration in 2009, taking liberal liberties with Émile Zola's novel *Thérèse Raquin* for the story of a country priest (Song Kang-ho, perhaps the finest Korean actor of his generation) who succumbs to long-simmering temptation after a bungled medical procedure turns him into a vampire. The degenerative aspect of vampirism moves to the fore in Park's unorthodox perspective on orthodoxy. The so-called Emmanuel Virus supersedes the good Catholic's most devoutly held pieties and spurs him to violate his celibacy vows in graphic fashion with his congregant's comely wife at his lowest moment of weakness. His affliction and resulting transgressions negotiate a broader tension between modernity (science, industrialization, change) and tradition (religion, nature, ceremony) not uncommon in Korea's national cinema.

Park puts his authorial stamp on the vampire mythology by means both aesthetic and thematic. Laying the groundwork he'd complete with his later feature *The Handmaiden*, he places his vampire in a swelteringly erotic yet coolly tasteful romance, a tone more prim than the seductress and more forwardly sexual than the heartthrob. In keeping with Park's uncanny atypicality, the verdant lushness of the village scenery draws a strong contrast with the usual sealed-off castles in need of a good dusting. Song's performance in the lead role breaks the most new ground, however; from moment to moment, he's in thrall of and frightened by his own capacity for sin.

Mexico — *Cronos*

Before Guillermo del Toro won the Oscar, before he became Hollywood's go-to guy for imaginative takes on musty old franchises, before everything, he made a small vampire picture in Mexico for a measly $2 million. His first feature effort reworked the mythology and thematic focus of the vampire tradition for an original variety of horror swaddled in a style fully-realized even on its creator's first outing. His version of vampiric infection is transmitted through the sting of a rare insect, trapped in a golden scarab-shaped medallion by an alchemist in the 16th century. In keeping with the creepy-crawly motif (the cockroach's indestructibility is the key to eternal life, it turns out), these vampires will occasionally shed their outermost layer of epidermis to reveal a ghostly white new skin beneath. For del Toro and the multiple characters scrambling to get a leg up on death, the vampire's most prized trait is its tenacity.

Working in moral shades of grey—the main character's last name is Gris, for crying out loud—del Toro strikes an elegiac, contemplative tone not often seen in the annals of horror. His chosen wretch, an observant but not quite devout antiques dealer, goes through the classically Catholic cycle of sin-penance-redemption, though del Toro leaves that last bit torturously unresolved. His final fade to white and the uncertainty it creates challenges its own expressions of faith, an internal conflict well-known to adherents of any strict religion.

Iran — *A Girl Walks Alone at Night*

The early promotion for Ana Lily Amirpour's debut foregrounded the globally-minded hybridization hardwired into its premise as a selling point, proudly declaring the 2014 film the first "Iranian feminist vampire Western." She sets her story in the fictitious Bad Town, a monochrome desert village informed by her magpie-collected subjects of fascination. (Though modelled after Iran, Bad Town is actually the SoCal city of Taft.) Amirpour cherry-picked stylistic signifiers from across North America, Europe and Asia for a mélange of styles and cool-kid shibboleths; you don't have to command a working knowledge of Sergio Leone, Jim Jarmusch, and Molly Haskell to appreciate the film, but it doesn't hurt. At an ecstasy-fuelled rave, attendees in all manner of referential costumes freely party as one, revelling in their motion; Amirpour's ethic as a curatorial artist functions similarly.

Her vampire, a nameless woman clad in a chador and never explicitly referred to as "vampire," lives a disaffected, bohemian lifestyle. In between bites, she kills time listening to records (vinyl fetishism being the purest example of Amirpour's prioritization of aesthetics over narrative practicality) and messing with locals. She stumbles into a reluctant romance with a neighborhood boy already involved in a domestic saga of his own, and just like the savage Coré in *Trouble Every Day*, she struggles to subdue her more violent impulses for the sake of love. But as the resigned final shot makes clear, the Girl lives only for herself. Amirpour has said the seed for this film began with the feeling of being like a bat while wearing her chador; with this film, she weaponizes her heritage and womanhood with a cultural and pop-cultural specificity.

Australia — *Outback Vampires*

The cinema of Australia has wrestled with tough questions about the country's troubled origins as a penal colony, the path to independence from the British Empire, and the white population's uneasy cohabitation with aboriginal peoples. *Outback Vampires* is not one of those films, but it does have a magical bouncing ball of guidance. Quietly shunted onto TV under the title *The Wicked*, Colin Eggleston's 1987 swan song contains one of the more impressive displays of unrestrained lunacy in the vampire canon. He didn't exactly reinvent the wheel in terms of story, or even his application of vampire concepts; two buddies and a telegenic female hitchhiker get waylaid at a creepy old mansion, where—surprise, surprise—the owners happen to be relatively average bloodsuckers.

There must be some unmentioned gas leak in the house, because the vampires in pursuit of our trio of heroes form but a single part in a larger onslaught of insanity. Inexplicable filtering and color-retouching, characters abruptly endowed with a crude facsimile of Spider-Man's powers, and a groanworthy sense of humor all add up to one glorious barrage of incoherence. Apropos of nothing, a rock band shreds through the fourth wall for a complete musical performance, as if in a music video. But for all its nuttier charms, Eggleston's film isn't all that imbued with a distinct Australian-ness. Though it could be said he translates the constant terror of being devoured by the country's Lovecraftian fauna into the unrelenting mayhem of his hell house.

Germany — *Vampyr*

Count Orlok casts a long shadow. It would seem that many viewers only have room in their heart for one early European vampire tour de force, judging from the higher profile enjoyed by *Nosferatu* while Carl Theodor Dreyer's 1932 feature remains the province of academics and more committed cinephiles. Though that's understandable: the Danish master's first foray into sound doesn't open itself up as willingly as Murnau's film. Dreyer liked to keep his audience at an arm's length and on their toes through disorienting artistic choices. He filled out his cast with non-professional actors, who would give more naturalistic performances than those performers trained by the restrictions of the stage and silent film to emote as hard as possible. He shot entirely on location, an unusual move in the age of the soundstage. And he photographed the film in a bleary soft focus, more closely resembling a weatherbeaten daguerreotype than a celluloid strip. Even on its first showings, the image already looked like a rediscovered antique.

The "vampyr" itself is far from Dreyer's focal point, not just in the film as a whole but in its efforts to generate fear. Dreyer dedicated more of his efforts to creating an atmosphere in which the vampire could exist than in establishing what would have been new mythology. Dreyer's vampire dies from a metal spike through the chest, a revelation tucked into a script entirely uninterested in the regimented pace of horror cinema. Even for a foreign film, Dreyer's magnum opus feels foreign; if *Vampyr* had emerged the box-office champion at the time of release, the whole of vampire cinema could have gone differently.

India — *Bandh Darwaza*

The booming Indian film industry embraced horror from its inception, but largely limited its purview to familiar faces from the national folklore: demons, spirits, witches and regionally specific monsters had free run of Bollywood for years. The first horror film containing a recognizably vampiric creature didn't come until 1990, and even then, he arrived flanked by a retinue of lackeys that audiences in India felt like they already knew and loved. (They are, incidentally, the best part of the film

— an old sorceress can turn her enemies' innards into poison.) Regardless, *Bandh Darwaza* and its splendid villain Neola opened up an entirely new corner of vampire civilization.

Logistically, the film plays it pretty fast and loose with vampire biology, but the inconsistencies and outright dismissals of reason make for unpredictable, thrilling cinema. Neola sports Dracula's defined widow's peak hairstyle, though his glowing red eyes and ever-present bulging forehead veins add a touch of Orlok's bestial energy. Neola possesses garden-variety hypnosis powers, but, more perplexingly, he shares Edward Cullen's capacity to impregnate human women the old-fashioned way. Much of this two-and-a-half-hour film, a notably lengthy run time for foam-and-rubber exploitation, revolves around Neola's efforts to procure a suitable heir, a quest that sidelines him for most of the film's second half while it slides into melodrama with spooky particulars. Neola's extended absence and the resulting mission drift allows the film to sneak in such standard components of a Bollywood blockbuster as an unrequited love, musical numbers, and a strapping hero. It's a dinner and a show, with a blood feast on the menu.

Japan — *Evil of Dracula*

O ne of the earliest fathers of Japanese horror cinema, Nobuo Nakagawa coined many of the tropes that persist in "J-horror" to this day. Many of the earliest features had a somewhat perfunctory relationship to vampire lore, simply containing this then-novel Western import, which mattered more to audiences than what the movie did with it. Nakagawa's 1959 feature *Lady*

Vampire actually starred a male vampire who only turned monstrous in the light of the moon, and 1968's *Goke, Body Snatcher From Hell* referred to its hematophagic (that is, blood-eating) aliens as vampires mostly for the sake of branding.

A trilogy of films directed by Mishio Yamamoto under the banner of the great Toho Studios fleshed out the profile of the Japanese vampire while ushering the national cinema into new depths (or are they heights?) of gore. The first, *Fear of the Ghost House: Bloodsucking Doll*, awkwardly splits the difference between the corporeal undead and the house-dwelling ghosts hailing from Japanese oral traditions on through to *The Ring*. The latter two interface more directly with the vampire, with the series hitting its stride in final installment *Evil of Dracula*. Somehow both Yamamoto's most audacious and balanced film, it wove the customs and visual signals of Japan (skin the color of clay from the earth, dark circles around the eyes) into a storyline informed by Bram Stoker's combination of woe and lust towards death. The cultural exchange inherent in the film also colors the story itself; vampirism comes to Japan as a European plague, a sound symbol for the steadfast threat of outside influence from white, imperialist powers.

China — *Mr. Vampire*

In Chinese folklore, it is said that preserved corpses from the Qing Dynasty will sometimes spring into action after resting dormant for centuries, feeding on life force, referred to as *qi*. You can spot a *jiangshi* from any number of telltale signs: they'll be clad in the customary 17th-century changshan shirt, they move with their arms outstretched (Western zombie fiction got it from them, not the other way around), and their sole method of locomotion is hopping. It is because this hopping looks deeply silly that most *jiangshi* movies ended up being comedies.

Chinese cinema had depicted the vampire as early as 1936 with Yeung Kung-Leung's little-seen *Midnight Vampire*, but the genre as it would most popularly be understood first took shape with Sammo Hung's 1980 feature *Close Encounters of the Spooky Kind*. Hung created a turducken of entertainment, jamming a slapstick comedy inside a horror flick, then cramming them both in a martial arts movie. He'd later bring his know-how to Ricky Lau's *Mr. Vampire* in 1985, working as a producer on the micro-genre's high-water mark. There's not much to distinguish the story from that of the other *jiangshi* films—a Taoist monk rouses and then must dispose of a hopper through a combination of spiritual disciplines and ass-kicking—but all the components that made them so diverting are in top form. Lam Ching-Ying can go blow for blow with Jackie Chan in his effortless excellence both as a clown and a fighter, and just as importantly, the extras playing his undead sparring partners can nimbly move through the choreography without dropping their act. Lustrous soundstage photography from Peter Ngor was just gravy in this delicacy.

The Philippines — *Blood Is the Color of Night*

Alternately released as *The Blood Drinkers* in the United States, this Filipino rarity strips the vampire film down to its barest elements and throws in a mad scientist for good measure. Though produced in 1964, the film has an undeveloped relationship to color, tinting each shot with a single hue in the fashion of early silent films. A shoestring budget necessitated other compromises, which amounted to a roughness of style not too far from the experimental. Director Gerardo de León slathered his cinematography with shadows to conceal the visible cheapness of his sets, but regardless, the cumulative effect creates unease by concealing enough visual information as to be de-stabilizing. It doesn't hurt that the English dub is exquisite nonsense, either; characters respond to questions with non sequiturs, and many speak as if they're in the middle of having a stroke.

The in-house vampire Dr. Marco lacks the pizzazz of his East Asian brethren or European predecessors, sadly. He's a man of science, and hilariously bad at his job, draining several townspeople as he frantically works towards a cure for his lover's sickness. He's been set up as a cue-balled Dracula with a slightly meatier face, outfitted with a cape that could have been taken from a unusually husky child's Halloween costume. In a distantly satisfying capacity, that Dr. Marco would be a dime-store version of himself fits in perfectly with the film's holistic chintziness.

Italy — *Blood for Dracula*

I n 1973, Paul Morrissey had just finished the seedy Italo-horror B-movie *Flesh for Frankenstein* and wanted to keep his momentum going. Working on the same set in the Villa Parisi just outside of Rome, he began pre-production on his follow-up the very next day. He wanted more of everything from *Blood for Dracula*; not just an increase in nudity and gristle, but to further push the boundaries of his own artistry and the medium. Operating in cahoots with his frequent collaborator

Andy Warhol (credited as a producer on the film), Morrissey crafted an uncommonly frisky work of Expressionism challenging norms on philosophical and visual fronts. Few vampire movies so enamored of pendulous bosoms also leave room to delve into the minutiae of Marxist theory.

The sublimely creepy Udo Kier played Dracula along the usual debonair lines, though his raging libido musses his tightly pressed hair more than usual. In this instance, Dracula can only subsist on the blood of a virgin, a device that leads to risqué farce before some surprising revelations about who's been sleeping with who trigger a massacre. Curlicues stick out at odd angles: legendary neorealist filmmaker Vittorio de Sica portrays a landowner who offers his daughters to Dracula after falling on hard times, and a mustachioed Roman Polanski cameos as a gambler at a local bar. Close-ups last longer than feels natural, or get so close as to feel invasive. Morrissey pushes his actors as far into the carnivalesque as they're willing to go, too. Kier's performance is the dead giveaway for this exploitation picture's loftier ambitions; his over-emoting is purposeful, an exaggeration drawing attention to the agonies of a character that had been turned into a Halloween novelty.

FURTHER READING AND VIEWING

1. *Vampires* (dir. John Carpenter, 1998)

2. *Buffy the Vampire Slayer* (dir. Fran Rubel Kuzui, 1992)

3. *Buffy the Vampire Slayer* (TV, 1997-2003)

4. *Leptirica* (dir. Dorde Kadijevic, 1973)

5. *Castlevania* (Video game series, 1986-present)

6. *True Blood* (TV, 2008-2014)

7. *The Monster Squad* (dir. Fred Dekker, 1987)

8. *Carmilla* (Joseph Sheridan Le Fanu, 1871)

9. *Dracula 2000* (dir. Patrick Lussier, 2000)

10. *The Velvet Vampire* (dir. Stephanie Rothman, 1971)

11. *Dark Shadows* (TV, 1965-1971)

12. *Bordello of Blood* (dir. Gilbert Adler, 1996)

13. *Dracula's Dog* (dir. Albert Band, 1973)

14. *Salem's Lot* (Steven King, 1975)

15. *Salem's Lot* (TV, 1979)

16. *Carpe Jugulum* (Terry Pratchett, 1998)

17. *Blood+* (TV, 2005-2006)

18. *The Vampyre* (John William Polidori, 1819)

19. *Fledgling* (Octavia Butler, 2005)

20. *The Munsters* (TV, 1964-1966)

21. *Razor Blade Smile* (dir. Jake West, 1998)

22. *Nocturna: Granddaughter of Dracula* (dir. Harry Hurwitz, 1979)

23. *The Strain* (TV, 2014-2017)

24. *The Vampire Tapestry* (Suzy McKee Charnas, 1980)

25. *Vampire Hunter D:Bloodlust* (dir. Yoshiaki Kawajiri, 2000)

ACKNOWLEDGEMENTS

Special thanks goes to my editor David Jenkins, who guided a perpetually frightened and confused writer through the longest and most involved professional project this young man had, at that point, ever undertaken. And who, with commendable delicacy, suggested that while Transmorphers jokes might be fun, they're still a little 'inside.'

For providing various professional resources instrumental in the writing of this book, thanks goes to Paula Mejia, Cady Drell, and Sophia Cross.

And for providing moral support during the process of researching and writing this book, thanks go to cherished friends and valuable sounding boards Stephen Schapero, Mara Frankel, Vikram Murthi, and Mallory Andrews; to my mother Michele and father Clint, whose regular inquiries as to how the book was coming along served as the most effective motivator to complete it; and to my sister Eva, who demanded this book be dedicated to her, and was eventually talked down into settling for a shout-out in the acknowledgements.

William Collins
An imprint of HarperCollinsPublishers
1 London Bridge Street
London SE1 9GF

www.WilliamCollinsBooks.com
First published in Great Britain by William Collins in 2018

1

A catalogue record for this book is
available from the British Library.

ISBN 978-0-00-825661-6

Series editors: David Jenkins, Tom Killingbeck, Clive Wilson
Cover illustration by Christopher DeLorenzo
Interior illustrations by Laurène Boglio
Design and layout: Oliver Stafford, Laurène Boglio, Sophie Mo

Printed and bound by CPI Group (UK) Ltd, Croydon, CR0 4YY